Adult Faith Practices

akaloo

AKALOO
ADULT FAITH PRACTICES

Writers: Seth Moland-Kovash, Rebecca M. Ninke, Martha E. Stortz,
    Carla Thompson Powell, Darryl Thompson Powell, and
    Megan Torgerson
Editor: Laurie J. Hanson
Interior design: Douglas Schmitz
Cover design: Spunk Design Machine
Illustrator: Ted Dawson

ISBN 978-0-8066-6065-3

Manufactured in U.S.A.

Contents

Introduction 1

Bible—How do I discover more about the Bible?

1. Practicing Faith 5
2. Daily Bible Reading 15
3. Meditation 25
4. Discernment 35
5. Spiritual Reading 45
6. The Lord's Prayer 55
7. Bible Study 65
8. Hearing God's Word in Worship 73

God—How do I experience God?

1. Centering Prayer 81
2. Silence 92
3. Gratitude 101
4. Sabbath Keeping 111
5. Baptism and Communion 121

Disciple—How do I live as a disciple?

1. Journaling 131
2. Confession and Repentance 141
3. Forgiveness 151
4. Giving 161
5. Humble Service 171

Church—How do we celebrate the life and mission of the church?

1. Prayer for Others   181
2. Worship   191
3. Encouragement   201
4. Celebration   209
5. Hospitality   217
6. Service in and through the Congregation   225
7. Testimony   233

World—How do we embrace the world?

1. Simplicity   241
2. Care of the Earth   251
3. Justice   261
4. Service to the Larger Community and World   271
5. Sharing the Story   281

Faith Practices Cards   back of book

Introduction

"Follow me," Jesus said to the first disciples. He invited them—not just once—but all along the way:

- "Follow me" (Matthew 9:9; Mark 2:14; Luke 5:27; John 1:43).
- "Follow me, and I will make you fish for people" (Matthew 4:19; Mark 1:17).
- "Take up [your] cross and follow me" (Matthew 16:24; Mark 8:34).
- "My sheep hear my voice. I know them, and they follow me" (John 10:27).
- "Whoever serves me must follow me" (John 12:26).

"Follow me," Jesus still says today. He invites us—not just once—but all along the way, every day of our lives. He invites us to follow him on the journey of discipleship.

Like the first disciples, we sometimes lose our way on this journey. We ignore Christ's daily invitation. We don't stay focused on the one we follow. We get off track.

Christians of all ages and times and places, however, have used *faith practices* as a compass on the journey of discipleship. These practices help us stay on track. They are opportunities, not requirements. They help us grow in faith, serve God, and follow Jesus. They are gifts for us to use, to stay focused on Christ. Through faith practices we constantly orient ourselves along the journey of discipleship.

The faith practices described in this course represent a small sample of practices Christians have used and found meaningful over time. Each unit in the course includes practices you can do on your own, practices you can share with others, and practices like corporate worship, where you join the communion of saints in their songs of ceaseless praise.

Some of these practices might be familiar to you, while others are not. You might already be doing a faith practice regularly. Maybe you need encouragement to keep faith practices going in your daily life. Maybe you've never been involved in any kind of faith practice. Whether you're a beginner or a long-time "practitioner," you can dive right into faith practices using the step-by-step coaching in each lesson!

Many people find it helpful and meaningful to build faith practices into their daily or weekly routines. Here are some ways the Faith Practices cards in this book can help you do that:

- Place the card for the week's lesson in your wallet, on a mirror, or in another location where you'll see it several times daily.
- Post a card on the refrigerator and use that faith practice at mealtimes.
- Use a card to explain a faith practice to family members or friends. Invite them to do the faith practice with you regularly.

- Pick a faith practice that you can do in a few minutes any time, anywhere, and keep that card handy each day.
- Leave a card on your pillow or beside your bed and use that faith practice at the end of the day.

Try out faith practices and make some of them a regular part of your life as you go through this course. Use them as a compass to follow Jesus on your journey of discipleship—the journey of a lifetime.

Testimony
1. Know your faith story.
2. Tell your f

Adult Faith Practices

Visit www.akaloo.org regularly for more information on faith practices and Akaloo.

CHURCH 7

Care of the Earth
1. Pray.
2. Consider what you can do.
3. Carry out earth-friendly practices.

Bible 1

How do I discover more about the Bible?

Practicing Faith

Key Text: Matthew 4:19
Key Idea: Faith practices offer a compass for the journey of discipleship—the journey of a lifetime.

BIBLE 1

Step-by-step: Practicing Faith

"Follow me." This is Jesus' invitation to the first disciples. It isn't just a onetime offer. These same words sustain

the disciples along the way. In fact, "follow me" are the first and last words Jesus speaks to Peter.

Jesus' invitation keeps coming to disciples today: "Follow me." This invitation comes to us in baptism, and it's reissued every day of our lives. Along the way, we need to stay focused on the one we follow. We need to listen for the invitation. We also need help to stay on track, even if we don't want to admit it.

Faith practices offer a compass for the journey of discipleship—the journey of a lifetime. Faith practices are actions done by Christians to grow in faith, serve God, and follow Jesus. They are not ways to work our way *up* to God—they are gifts disciples use to stay focused on Christ. They have been used by Christians of all ages and times and places. Through faith practices we constantly orient ourselves along the journey of discipleship.

The faith practices described in this course represent a small sample of practices Christians have used and found meaningful over time. Some of these practices might be familiar to you while others might not. You might already be doing a faith practice regularly. Maybe you need encouragement to keep faith practices going in your daily life. Maybe you've never been involved in any kind of faith practice. Whether you're a beginner or a long-time practitioner, you can dive right into faith practices using the step-by-step coaching in each lesson!

BIBLE 1

Each unit in this course starts out with practices you can do on your own, moves to practices you can share with others, and builds to practices like corporate worship, where you join the communion of saints in their songs of ceaseless praise. All of these faith practices start with the invitation "Follow me" and point us toward the one we follow: Jesus Christ, the Son of God.

As you go through this course, try out the faith practices that are explained in the lessons. You might find that different practices encourage you or appeal to you at different times of the year, and even at different times in your life. Consider adopting a practice with your family or group of friends. Think about which practice(s) you might want to make part of your own daily or weekly routine.

 Do It Yourself: *Look and listen for Jesus' invitation to you: "Follow me!"*

 Every day we receive invitations and messages to follow someone or something—a certain guru, leader, or expert, a diet or exercise program, or a brand or lifestyle. Who or what do you follow?

Follow Me

The words "Follow me!" begin and end the journey of discipleship. These are the first words Jesus says to Peter, and Peter drops his nets to follow (Matthew 4:18-20). These are the last words Jesus says to Peter, too (John 21:1-19). In between these first and last words, Peter follows Jesus. There are high points and low points in his story. Peter reaches the lowest point as Jesus is led away to be crucified, when—not once, but three times—Peter denies ever knowing Jesus.

Peter isn't the only one who struggles with discipleship. After Jesus dies and rises again, the other disciples get lost, too. Aimless and unmoored, they return to their old lives. Jesus finds several of them fishing and he begins to cook breakfast. This "First Breakfast" echoes the Last Supper. Before his crucifixion Jesus tells the disciples to remember him in the breaking of the bread; after his resurrection Jesus reminds the disciples they are still on a journey.

At the First Breakfast Jesus engages Peter in conversation: "Do you love me?" Peter says, "Yes!" but Jesus persists in asking, "Do you love me?" Peter's response intensifies as his frustration mounts, but each "Yes!" erases one of his denials of Jesus. When Jesus finishes his gentle interrogation, he reissues his call: "Follow me." All Peter has to say is "Yes!" Jesus' invitation reorients Peter to the journey of discipleship.

Peter's story is ours, too. How do we follow a risen Lord? It was hard enough when Jesus was around. The disciples got lost when Jesus was in their midst. Where do we find Jesus after the resurrection? How do we stay focused on Jesus? Faith practices such as the ones in this unit (daily Bible reading, meditation, discernment, spiritual reading, the Lord's prayer, study, and hearing the word in worship) offer a compass for the journey ahead, orienting us again and again to the journey of discipleship.

 What helps you stay on track when you go somewhere? What helps you stay on track as you follow Jesus?

The Marks of Christ

Christ's crucified and resurrected body was marked. There were wounds where the nails entered his hands and feet, and another wound where the sword pierced his side.

St. Francis of Assisi was a man who chose to live a simple monastic life. After a long night of fasting and prayer, it is said that he saw a vision of the crucified Christ and received in his own body the marks that were on Christ's. The date was September 14, 1224. St. Francis bore these marks (called the *stigmata*) from the night he received them until his death on October 3, 1226.

People today mark themselves with piercings and tattoos, clothes and hairstyles. How do you mark yourself? How are you marked as a "child of God"?

The Marks of the church

The church—the body of Christ in the world—is marked, just as Christ's crucified and resurrected body was marked. According to Martin Luther, sixteenth-century reformer and founder of the Lutheran faith tradition, the people of God are marked by a series of faith practices.

These marks are a compass that helps Christians locate the body of Christ in the world. Luther maintained that wherever people are preaching and hearing the word, baptizing, sharing the Lord's Supper, forgiving, calling out leaders, praying/praising/teaching, and walking the discipleship journey, there is the body of Christ in the world.

BIBLE 1

Wrap-up

Jesus issues the invitation to us: "Follow me." It's not just a onetime offer. He speaks these words of invitation and encouragement all along the way. Following Jesus on the journey of discipleship is the journey of a lifetime. Faith practices offer a compass for the road ahead; they keep us on track.

In the next lesson we begin closely looking at—and experiencing—a variety of faith practices. The first one, daily Bible reading, encourages us to let God's word "dwell" in us (Colossians 3:16).

Peter was one of the most clueless of the disciples, particularly in Mark's gospel. He wanted Jesus to be a revolutionary leader, liberating the Jews from Roman occupation. He let Jesus know this—in no uncertain terms. Jesus rebuked him sharply, calling him "Satan." Yet Jesus never told Peter, "Get lost." He simply said, "Get behind me." There was still a journey, and Peter was still on it.

If there's hope for Peter, there's hope for us.

In My Life

- Find a way to remind yourself *whose* you are by remembering your baptism each day. Put a bowl of water on your kitchen or dining room or bedside table. Each time you pass by that table, take time to dip your fingers in the water and make the sign of the cross on your forehead.
- Take a business card and write under your name, "Child of God." Turn it over and write on the back, "Follow me." If you don't have a business card, make one. Keep it in a place where you can see it throughout the day.
- Look and listen for Jesus' daily invitation: "Follow me."
- Invite someone to join you in taking this course.
- Make arrangements to meet with another person weekly during this course to try out the faith practices and discuss them together. Your "practice partner" might be someone else taking the course, a close friend or coworker, or a family member.

BIBLE 1

Bible 2

How do I discover more about the Bible?

Daily Bible Reading

Key Text: Colossians 3:16
Key Idea: Daily Bible reading is the practice of reading deep into the word of God—and letting it read us.

Step-by-step: Daily Bible Reading

Preparation: Find a regular time when you can be alone with God's word. Also find a regular place, anywhere in your home, workplace, or other surroundings—a chair, sofa, kitchen table, stoop, or the trunk of a tree.

Tools and materials: a Bible and a list of daily readings (You can find daily Bible readings in hymnals, devotionals, and Bibles. Also check your denomination's Web site for reading lists or daily texts.)

Time: 20–30 minutes or more suggested

1 Sit in silence for a few minutes. Imagine all of your thoughts and worries running out of your mind. Let your heart fill with God's blessing in return.

DIY This practice is about *daily* reading, not *lots of* reading. As the practice becomes more familiar, you may find yourself reading less, but reading more deeply.

2 Read the texts for the day, savoring them like a good meal. The following exercises may help.

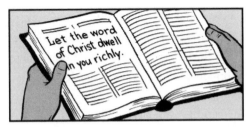

• **Role-play:** Imagine yourself as each of the characters and notice how this cracks open the meaning of the text.

• **Paraphrase:** Imagine that you are writing the text and then preaching it to others. In a few simple phrases or sentences, what would you say?

• **Emphasize—and re-emphasize:** Read a passage repeatedly, stressing different words each time.

3 Close by praising and thanking God.

 In which times and places can you focus on God, free of distractions and interruptions?

The Mind of Christ

The apostle Paul writes to his beloved community at Philippi: "Let the same mind be in you that was in Christ Jesus" (Philippians 2:5). How is it possible for us to know or possess the mind of Christ?

Unlike many people around him, Jesus could read. And as a Jewish boy he knew the Hebrew scriptures backwards and forwards. We catch a glimpse of him doing his daily reading in one of the synagogues in his homeland of Galilee (Luke 4:16-19). Luke tells us it was Jesus' "custom" to be in the synagogue on the Sabbath. Jesus unrolls the scroll to a passage in Isaiah (61:1-2) and reads:

> *The Spirit of the Lord is upon me,*
> *because he has anointed me to bring good news to*
> *the poor.*
> *He has sent me to proclaim release to the captives*
> *and recovery of sight to the blind,*
> *to let the oppressed go free,*
> *to proclaim the year of the Lord's favor.*
> *Luke 4:18-19*

Then Jesus tells the congregation: "Today this scripture has been fulfilled in your hearing" (Luke 4:21). The people should be delighted, but instead they mock him. They cannot imagine that God would work through someone so ordinary in someplace so undistinguished as their own.

Still, the text that Jesus read came true in his life. As Jesus read this text and others, the Bible read him, confirming his own walk with God. Jesus challenges the Pharisees, drawing on other words from Isaiah: "This people honors

me with their lips, but their hearts are far from me. . ." (Mark 7:6; Isaiah 29:13). And when called to identify himself, Jesus draws from scripture to make himself known (for examples, see Daniel 7:13-14 and Isaiah 42:1-4; 49:1-6; 50:4-11; 52:13—53:12). Even as he dies on the cross, Jesus speaks words from scripture: "My God, my God, why have you forsaken me?" (Psalm 22:1).

Jesus not only read scripture regularly, it was very familiar to him. To become familiar with the mind of Christ, then, we become familiar with scripture. We follow this practice that Jesus followed.

 Jesus doesn't ask us to do anything that he hasn't already done, or go any place where he hasn't already been. Does this make it easier or more difficult to follow him? Why?

Spreading the Word

Many of us have easy access to the Bible today. We can download the entire Bible—in almost any language we want—from the Internet, or load scripture passages into a personal digital assistant (PDA). We can carry a pocket-sized Bible with us while traveling, or find a Bible in the drawer of a hotel room. We might even have several different versions of the Bible in our homes or church libraries.

In Jesus' time, things were very different. For one thing, few people were actually literate, so anyone who *could* read, read aloud for the benefit of others. Second, producing copies of sacred texts took a great deal of time and effort. Scribes laboriously copied the scriptures of the Hebrew people. These texts were then rolled onto long scrolls. Because of the hard work involved in producing the scrolls, the scriptures were treated with honor and respect. The daily reading in the synagogue involved an elaborate ritual. The rabbi blessed the reader, who in turn blessed the text.

What can you or your congregation do about people or places today that don't have access to a Bible? How can you remind yourself not to take the Bible for granted?

Captive to God's Word: Terry Anderson

On March 16, 1985, Associated Press correspondent Terry Anderson was abducted in the streets of Beirut, thrown into the trunk of a car, and taken to a secret location. He spent the next six years and nine months held captive by the Shiite Hezbollah militants.

At times Anderson and others held captive with him were treated well; at times a guard would hold a gun to their temples and threaten to pull the trigger. The psychological torture was demoralizing, but it had a strange effect on Anderson. Someone in his situation could easily have dissolved into despair or rage. Instead, Anderson began to reflect on his life, particularly the times when he had wronged others. In these terrifying circumstances, Anderson found Sabbath time and a Sabbath place.

Anderson, a lapsed Roman Catholic, made his first confession in 25 years when he heard that one of the other captives was a priest. When he finished, he and the priest were both in tears. Anderson asked for a Bible, and his captors found him one. Over the years he read and reread the Bible, cover to cover, memorizing large portions of it.

BIBLE 2

The word of Christ dwelled richly within Anderson. As he read the biblical stories, they read him. They showed him he was not alone in his abandonment; they offered him hope. They showed him a world that could be different.

Like Anderson, Martin Luther was captivated by the Bible. When asked to recant his writings at the Diet of Worms in 1521, Martin Luther said, "My conscience is captive to the Word of God." For Terry Anderson, being captive to God's word brought joy—and changed his life.

Wrap-up

Everyone needs direction on the journey of discipleship. Daily Bible reading is the practice of reading deep into the word of God—and letting it read us.

The next practice, meditation, trains us to be still and listen for God. It allows the word of God to take root in us.

Daily Bible reading gives daily direction on the journey of discipleship. As long as Jesus is in front of you, you're on the right path.

In My Life

- Commit yourself to reading the Bible each day in the coming week. If daily Bible reading is something new for you, start out with a few minutes each day and gradually add to the time you spend dwelling in God's word.
- Remember that faith practices are not requirements to receive God's love and grace but tools to help us grow in relationship with God and one another.
- Look for daily Bible readings on the Internet. At the Evangelical Lutheran Church in America's Web site (www.elca.org), for example, you can read daily Bible texts online, sign up to have them sent to your e-mail address, or set them up on a PDA.
- If you simply can't keep to your regularly scheduled daily Bible reading, take time to pray. You might use a prayer like this: Dear God, today is more than I can manage. I know I can trust you to find me in all the busyness today. Behold me and bless me, and may I behold and bless others this day. Amen.

BIBLE 2

How do I discover more about the Bible?

Meditation

Key Text: Psalm 46:10

Key Idea: As we rest in the word of God in meditation, the word of God rests in us and fills us with God's peace.

Step-by-step: Meditation

Preparation: Find a regular time and a regular place where you can sit quietly, alone with the word of God.
Tools and materials: a Bible and daily readings or a verse you have committed to read for the week
Time: 20–30 minutes suggested

Ideally, meditation follows daily reading. Here's how:

1 Receive God's word: After you have sat with the texts for the day, ask yourself what phrase had an impact on you.

2 Repeat God's word: Say the phrase over and over again. Synchronize repetition of the words with your breathing, so that you are literally breathing them in, breathing them out. Think of this as the Holy Spirit working in and through you. Let God's word dwell deeply in you. Then breathe out in blessing.

3

Rest in the word and God: Repeat a smaller phrase or word over and over again. This is God's word *for you, for now,* and *for life.* Finally, rest in God's presence.

4

Return: After you have rested in God for a while, come back to your word; come back to the verse of scripture you chose. Thank God for being with you.

With its focus on regular, steady breathing, meditation relaxes us. Don't worry if you fall asleep. Sleep leaves us at our most vulnerable—we rest in God's arms and depend utterly on God's care.

What do you do when conversation lags? Do you try to fill the silence with words? Can you sit easily in silence with anyone? With yourself?

The Grace of Abiding

Mark's gospel gets out of the gate with a shot, beginning with Jesus' baptism and propelling him into action. Count the number of times the first chapter of Mark's gospel uses the word "immediately." Mark portrays Jesus at a gallop, and his ministry starts with a flurry of healings and exorcisms, miracles and teachings.

Yet even in Mark's gospel Jesus takes time out, not just once but often (Mark 6:46; 9:2; 14:32). He ascends a mountaintop to pray; he escapes from the crowds into a deserted place to be alone. Jesus, too, needed his Sabbath times and his Sabbath places. In the practice of meditation we are finding time and place to do what he did—abide in the word.

Indeed, Jesus offers his disciples a kind of guided meditation in John 15:1-11. The passage comes from what scholars call Jesus' "farewell discourse." He knows his time on earth is coming to a close, and he wants to give the disciples a way of staying connected to him—even in death. Read the passage over aloud and in silence.

Notice how often the word "abide" is used in this passage. For this word to be repeated—and repeated so consciously!— must mean something. Jesus wants the disciples to live in him, remaining in his word and resting in his love.

Now look at how important listening is to this whole practice. Jesus invites us to *abide* in his words, and for the words to sink in, we need first to hear them. When he speaks of keeping his commandments, he signals another important form of listening: obedience. He develops this in the teaching that immediately follows: "You are my friends if you do what I command you" (John 15:14). Obeying Jesus' commandments involves listening for his invitation to follow. The Latin derivation puts this forcefully: "obedience" comes from the root words *ob-* + *-audire*, literally, "to listen for" someone or something. In allowing God's word to fill us, we are filled with listening.

Finally, Jesus promises that this kind of obedience fills us—not with dread or duty—but with joy. When we truly fill with the things Jesus has said to us, we fill with joy.

Meditation invites us into the presence of God, "so that my joy may be in you, and that your joy may be complete" (John 15:11).

Did You Know?

• Meditation is practiced across cultures and religions. In some cases, people use different techniques or direct their attention toward different objects, but rhythmic breathing, deep focus, and a sense of connection to something beyond us are part of meditation throughout the world's religions. The prevalence of this practice suggests a common human hunger for the divine.

 What do you need to empty out of your life to make room for God's word and Christ's joy?

Unlimited Refills

God's word never runs dry. It promises to quench our thirst with living water. But we can only fill our cups if they are first empty.

Not every time of prayer, Bible reading, and meditation is a mountaintop experience. The great spiritual writers spoke of dry times in prayer. Benedict of Nursia (circa 480–550), founder of the The Rule of St. Benedict, promised low points beyond the high points or "first fervor of conversion." John of the Cross (1542–1591) wrote from his own painful experience of "the dark night of the soul." Martin Luther reflected his own experience of spiritual dryness in counsel to his barber. There were times when he could neither pray nor meditate. At those times, he directed his friends to pick him up and carry him into the church, so that he could be surrounded by the prayers of others.

Did You Know?

• Like all faith practices, meditation is a way of "showing up," and as a wise person put it, that's what life is all about. Some days there are fireworks, but mostly it's just ordinary time. You show up, because it's what you do, it's who you are. And over time you grow used to resting in the word. And it grows used to resting in you.

It is tempting to interpret dryness in faith practices as abandonment by God, but the great spiritual writers counsel otherwise. This dryness is a way of emptying our cups, so that God might fill them again.

Martin Luther reportedly had his favorite scriptural passages written on scraps of paper and pinned to his bedroom wall. What could you do to remind yourself, even when there is dryness in your spiritual life, that God's word never runs dry?

A Life of Prayer and Meditation: Julian of Norwich

Little is known of Julian of Norwich (circa 1342–1416). Even her proper name is uncertain. She was born in the middle of the fourteenth century and at some point she became an "anchoress," a solitary vowed religious woman who established her residence or "anchorage" in a small cottage attached to St. Julian's Church in the wealthy cloth-trading city of Norwich near the North Sea of England. The ritual committing Julian to her anchorage combined elements of the burial service with the service of holy matrimony. At once, she became a bride of Christ, dedicating herself to him; simultaneously, she became dead to the world, for she never left her anchorage again.

Julian dedicated her life to prayer and meditation. When she was a young woman of about thirty, she fell gravely ill, and during her illness she meditated on Christ's passion and suffering. She had a series of sixteen personal revelations, which she describes as both physical and spiritual visions of the dying Lord.

It was a time of plague in the city, and people around her were dying. Miraculously, Julian recovered. Having been blessed with such powerful revelations, Julian breathed them

BIBLE 3

out in blessing. She wrote down a short version of her revelations immediately upon her recovery, but she continued to meditate on her visions for the next twenty years. She then wrote a longer version of these *Showings* or *Revelations of Divine Love*. Both texts describe her vision, along with her reflection on them. These texts stand alongside Geoffrey Chaucer's *Canterbury Tales* as classics of writing in Middle English.

Julian's works are also a spiritual classic. After years of meditating on Christ's passion, she discovered the blessed assurance that "All will be well." Christ's suffering and death is not only judgment for sin, it is evidence of love. This was Julian's inescapable conclusion, and she closed her visions and reflections with extraordinary testimony to God's love.

Wrap-up

Meditation follows naturally from daily reading, as we let the word of God fill us and take root in our soul. Filled with the Spirit of God in Christ Jesus, we are better able to discern other spirits that cross our lives.

The next lesson will focus on the practice of discernment, which forms, informs, and transforms us by the living word of God.

 When your mind gets distracted during meditation time (and it will), relax and return to thinking about your word, phrase, or passage from scripture.

In My Life

- Select one of the following texts: "Be still, and know that I am God" (Psalm 46:10), "As the Father has loved me, so I have loved you; abide in my love" (John 15:9), or "All will be well" (Julian of Norwich). Sit with that text for up to 15 minutes each day during this week. Rest in the word.
- Instead of folding your hands for prayer, keep them open as a reminder that you are receiving God's word. To receive it, you have to let go of everything else that you hold on to so tightly: money, success, and certain images and illusions of yourself.
- As you meditate on a Bible text, repeat a phrase over and over again, slowing your breathing to the cadence of the words, letting them calm you. Then try repeating it in smaller and smaller parts:
  "Be still and know that I am God."
  "Be still and know that I am."
  "Be still and know."
  "Be still."
  "Be."
- After you rest in the word, resurface by building up the Bible text:
  "Be."
  "Be still."
  "Be still and know."
  "Be still and know that I am."
  "Be still and know that I am God."
- Remember that faith practices are gifts from God to help us grow in discipleship.

Bible 4

How do I discover more about the Bible?

Discernment

Key Text: 1 John 4:1
Key Idea: In the practice of discernment we draw on God's word and the Spirit's guidance to deal with real-life decisions and issues.

BIBLE 4

Step-by-step: Discernment

Preparation: Find a regular time and a regular place in the midst of each day where you can sit quietly. You will also need a trusted friend or counselor.
Tools and materials: a Bible and daily readings or a verse you have committed to read for the week
Time: 20–30 minutes or more

1 Get the facts: Gather up all the information you can. Consider how the situation looks to God and the various people involved in it.

2 Consider your desires: What do you really want to do? You might decide not to move in the direction of your desires, but take time to identify them.

Look for God in the situation: Ask yourself, where is God in all of this? You might be surprised by how God meets you, but be certain that God will be there.

Think about the outcome and the fruit it will bear: On the basis of the best information you have, along with your most faithful discernment of where your hearts is and where God is leading you, project possible scenarios and how they affect you, others, and the world.

DIY There is not a set process for discernment, but it generally includes the four steps shown here.

Discernment involves listening to your own heart, to a pastor or counselor or friend, and to God. How well do you listen?

The Fruit of the Spirit

The practice of discernment invites the Holy Spirit to direct our lives, but how do we recognize that direction?

Because God works in the particulars of each life and each situation, there are no easy ways to measure for this or formulas that work in every situation. The Spirit works differently in one life than in another. Most often, however, we discern the work of the Spirit by its effects.

The apostle Paul offers timeless counsel on the working of the Spirit. He advises the Galatians to judge a situation by its fruit. He describes the effects of the working of the flesh: "fornication, impurity, licentiousness, idolatry, sorcery, enmities, strife, jealousy, anger, quarrels, dissensions, factions, envy, drunkenness, carousing, and things like these" (Galatians 5:19-20). By all counts, these are unhappy endings to any story.

Paul then lists nine effects of the work of the Spirit: "By contrast, the fruit of the Spirit is love, joy, peace, patience, kindness, generosity, faithfulness, gentleness, and self-control" (Galatians 5:22-23). It's important to see that Paul speaks in the singular. These are not nine different "fruits"; they are a single "fruit." In a very real sense, the Spirit's working is unified.

There's something else going on here as well. The Spirit focuses on three different relationships: our relationship to

God, our relationship to others, and our relationship to ourselves. Love, joy, and peace link us to God. They are like a compass pointing us to the true north. Patience, kindness, and generosity ground our relationships to others. They translate love, joy, and peace into the language of human contact. Finally, the Spirit shows us our best selves in the virtues of faithfulness, meekness, and self-control.

Did You Know?

• The prophet Jeremiah reminds us that not all desires should be honored: "The heart is devious above all else; it is perverse—who can understand it?" (Jeremiah 17:9).

The fruit of the Spirit binds us to relationships with God, the neighbor, and the self. The process of discernment consciously considers the impact of a decision on each of these touchstones.

 What factors have you usually considered when you make an important decision? How would your decisions be affected if you took God, your neighbor, and yourself into consideration?

It Takes Time

Ignatius Loyola (circa 1491–1556), founder of the Society of Jesus, was convinced God leads us through our desires. Making the right decision or taking the right path, he believed, left a Christian with a sense of *confirmation* or being at peace with oneself and the decision. On the other hand, making a bad decision or taking the wrong path left a Christian with a sense of *desolation* or being restless, heartsick, and ill at ease.

Of course, that's great Monday morning quarterbacking! How do you play Sunday's game, not knowing how you'll feel the next day? Ignatius underscored the importance of making decisions slowly, taking time to imagine possible outcomes. A quick decision—or pressure to make a quick decision—is almost always a signal that something is not right.

Did You Know?

• The apostle Paul gives a word of caution about the temptation to always do one more thing and put ourselves at risk of excessive stress and burnout. Paul puts it well: "Even Satan disguises himself as an angel of light" (2 Corinthians 11:14).

 How much time do you take to make an important decision? How much time would you like to take?

Discerning the Spirit: Teresa of Avila

Teresa of Avila (1515–1582) grew up in Catholic Spain and entered a Carmelite convent at the age of 20. For almost 20 years, she struggled with prayer, finding her prayer life arid and unrewarding. At the age of 49 she had a powerful conversion experience, which showed her what was wrong: she'd been trying too hard. She gave her prayer over to God, letting it be God's work rather than her own.

This new experience of God brought with it many visions, and a cadre of spiritual directors were sent in to help Teresa discern the spirits. The first round of directors was convinced her extraordinary experiences were satanic: they did not come from the Spirit of God in Christ. Finally a new director believed in the validity of her experiences and directed her to focus on the passion of Christ.

Teresa went on to reform her order and write texts of spiritual direction. Her writings remain among the great spiritual classics.

Wrap-up

Discernment draws on the practices of daily Bible reading and meditation, bringing the word of God into contact with real-life decisions and issues. It shows us the Spirit is on the move in our lives.

The next practice, spiritual reading, invites us to use the examples of the saints—living and dead—in following the Spirit's leading in our own lives.

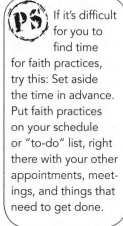

PS If it's difficult for you to find time for faith practices, try this: Set aside the time in advance. Put faith practices on your schedule or "to-do" list, right there with your other appointments, meetings, and things that need to get done.

In My Life

- Discuss an important issue with someone you trust. Commit to talking this issue over with all parties involved in your decision, so that as you role-play their responses, you have some hard evidence to go on. Take time to imagine yourself into possible outcomes. Are you left with feelings of desolation or consolation?
- Be of help to someone in need of discernment. Ask four questions: What's going on? Where's your heart? Where's God in the midst of this? How would this bear fruit—and what fruit would it bear?
- Identify one or two trusted friends or a pastor or spiritual director who can advise you regularly as part of your practice of discernment.
- Teach this practice to a teen dealing with a challenge or decision. Be available to listen as he or she goes through the discernment process.

Bible 5

How do I discover more about the Bible?

Spiritual Reading

Key Text: 1 John 1:3-4

Key Idea: Through spiritual reading we look into the lives of other disciples—living and dead—discover testimonies of faith, and receive encouragement to write about and live a Spirit-filled life.

BIBLE 5

Step-by-step: Spiritual Reading

Preparation: Set aside a time and place.
Tools and materials: the story of a saint or disciple that interests you, a journal, and a pen or pencil
Time: a few minutes at a time or more

1 Read the story of another Christian on a journey of discipleship, a chapter or two each day if possible. To sort out what you read, you might ask these questions:

- What's going on?
- Where's this disciple's heart?
- Where did this disciple find God in all this?
- How would this life bear fruit—and what fruit did it bear?

2 Write in your journal about what you've learned. Take notes for your own story of discipleship. Where has scripture shaped your life? Where has the Spirit led you?

? *What turned your life to the journey of discipleship? How would you communicate that to others?*

 DIY There are many different kinds of spiritual reading and Spirit-filled writing: autobiography, counsel and direction, poetry, essay, commentaries on books of scripture, songs, hymns, and spiritual songs. Try out different types of reading and writing, or stick with one that's meaningful to you.

Sharing Joy

Jesus had warned the disciples over and over again that he would leave them, but still they weren't ready for his ascension when it happened. Reformation artist Albrecht Dürer captured their dismay in a woodcut. The woodcut depicts all the disciples scattered in disarray at the bottom of the picture—some are reaching into the heavens, while others simply stare at the clouds in disbelief. At the top of the picture are two feet hanging out of some clouds. The rest of Jesus has risen beyond the frame of the cutting. You can almost hear the angels scolding the disciples: "Men of Galilee, why do you stand looking up towards heaven?" (Acts 1:11).

Imagine what else the angels might have said: "Hey, you guys! Snap out of it. You're not going to spend the rest of your lives peering off into another world. There's *this* world to take care of. Your ministry begins now. Your ministry begins here. Stop cloud-gazing and get to work!"

And the disciples did get to work, establishing communities of faith, passing on Jesus' teachings, healing, and working miracles. The Acts of the Apostles read as the Acts of the Holy Spirit—the Spirit of the risen Christ worked because of and in spite of the band of disciples.

The disciples expected Jesus to return in their lifetimes and nurtured their communities on that expectation. There was no time to write anything down. Paul discouraged Christians from marrying. If he could, he would have forbidden them from buying green bananas. Jesus was coming—and soon!

But Jesus didn't come back when these early followers thought he would. By 60 A.D. they began to die, most of them killed by persecution. Peter and Paul were executed. The people who knew Jesus best were no longer around. Who would tell their stories?

People began to hunker down for the long haul, organizing their communities more tightly against the ravages of time and persecution. They ritualized elements of worship that had been more spontaneous; they put their faith in the words of basic creeds; they elected leaders who were representatives of the original disciples. Most importantly, they began to tell the stories that the disciples had told them about Jesus. They added to these stories about the disciples themselves.

In these stories, early believers found the joy they had expected to find upon Jesus' return. That joy was not dampened or erased; it was just rechanneled. They wrote to reach out for Jesus. The practice of Spirit-filled writing was born. The practice of spiritual reading began.

 Who was instrumental in telling you the stories of Jesus and the disciples?

BIBLE 5

Discipleship Is Contagious

In the early church there were more than the four Gospels that we know today. Around 200 A.D. a document from Rome, known as the Muratorian Canon, listed writings in an order that we recognize as the New Testament. These writings were "official" story. Other writings were recommended as helpful to disciples, such as The Shepherd of Hermas, The Gospel of Peter, and The Apocalypse of Peter. Still other writings were rejected outright as heretical, including the "gnostic" gospels.

Whether they were accepted into the canon or not, whether they were condemned as heretical or not, the writers of all of these texts shared a goal: to get the word out. They told stories of Jesus and stories of the people who followed him. The writers intended to mentor, encourage, and inspire future generations of disciples. In the telling, they hoped to make Christ present in the communities of faith that followed them.

These Spirit-filled writings show us there is something about discipleship that is contagious. You can't help but share it. Witness is not so much a duty but a joy. As we read Spirit-filled writings, we share in that joy. When we tell our own stories, we share that joy with others.

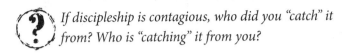

If discipleship is contagious, who did you "catch" it from? Who is "catching" it from you?

A Spirit-filled Writer: Thomas Merton

Seeking more in life than an endless round of jazz clubs, bars, and women, Thomas Merton (1915–1968) sought out Hindu monk Mahanambrata Brahmachari. If Merton hoped to be taken on as a disciple, he was sorely disappointed. Brahmachari pointed Merton instead to his own spiritual roots, in particular Augustine's *Confessions* and the medieval spiritual classic *The Imitation of Christ.* Surprised that the Hindu sage would direct him to Christian spiritual reading, Merton nonetheless followed this advice. The spiritual reading drew him back to prayer.

The capstone of Merton's return to faith was a book on the conversion of Jesuit priest and poet Gerard Manley Hopkins. Merton suddenly saw himself following that same path. He arranged immediately to meet with a priest, and within weeks was studying the catechism and learning the basics of the faith. He was baptized at age 23.

Merton became a Trappist monk at 26. Encouraged to write, he did just that, becoming an enormously popular writer. His spiritual autobiography, *The Seven Storey Mountain,* inspired others to renewed their spiritual commitments.

BIBLE 5

Merton's spiritual reading inspired him to do his own spirit-filled writing, which then became spiritual reading for still others.

Wrap-up

Spiritual reading allows us to learn about the Spirit's work in the lives of other disciples, living and dead. These stories can inspire us and encourage us to share our own stories of faith with others.

In the next faith practice, prayer, we breathe in the Holy Spirit—and breathe out blessing.

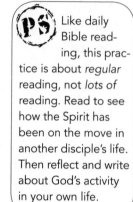

Like daily Bible reading, this practice is about *regular* reading, not *lots of* reading. Read to see how the Spirit has been on the move in another disciple's life. Then reflect and write about God's activity in your own life.

In My Life

- Resolve to do some spiritual reading this week and pay attention to what strikes you about the life of this person. If you wish, write a letter that this person might write to you, full of advice and affection for you.
- Resolve to do some spirit-filled writing of your own this week. You may want to try commentary on scripture, poetry, journaling, or something else.
- Find some friends who enjoy spiritual reading and make arrangements to meet regularly to discuss a book of your choice. Another option: Find some friends who enjoy spiritual writing and make arrangements to meet regularly to share portions of your journals.

How do I discover more about the Bible?

The Lord's Prayer

Key Text: Luke 11:1-13
Key Idea: The Lord's Prayer teaches us how to pray, what to pray for, and where God wants us to serve.

Step-by-step: The Lord's Prayer

Preparation: Have a time and place set aside, or pray with a group or a congregation.
Tools and materials: none
Time: difficult to measure, because the prayer is lived out each day

1 Name God: The Lord's Prayer names God as "our Father." In this prayer Jesus speaks God's name in this most intimate form of address. Moreover, Jesus reminds us that "our Father" has many children.

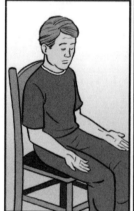

2 Praise God: Bless God for who God is and what God has done: "Hallowed be your name." Also embrace God's will and God's kingdom: "Your kingdom come, your will be done."

3 Ask God: Petition God for what people need. The Lord's Prayer asks for food, forgiveness, and freedom from temptation: "Give us today our daily bread. Forgive us our sins as we forgive those who sin against us. Save us from the time of trial and deliver us from evil."

4 Bless God: The Lord's Prayer begins in praise and ends in blessing: "For the kingdom, the power, and the glory are yours, now and forever."

> **DIY** The Lord's Prayer gives a basic pattern for all prayer: naming, praising, asking, blessing, and letting it be so. This basic pattern can be used in every prayer.

FOOD DONATIONS

5 Let it be so: *Amen* means literally "let it be so." It is Jesus' call to feed people who are hungry, extend hospitality to people we don't know, and honor friends in need. Consider where in the day ahead you can enact this prayer and answer this call.

? *What part of the Lord's Prayer is easiest for you to pray? What part is the most difficult for you to pray? Why?*

The Prayer Jesus Taught

The Lord's Prayer is taught in Sunday, recited in worship, and prayed by many church groups and families. Still, it's possible to race through it so quickly we don't know or remember what we're actually saying.

Let's slow things down and look at each petition of the Lord's Prayer, because here we see God's intentions for us.

"Our Father": Every prayer begins with naming the God in whom "we live and move and have our being" (Acts 17:28). Jesus gives the disciples a radical way to address God—the direct and intimate name of "Abba" or "Father." The qualifier "in heaven" sets this Father apart from earthly fathers.

"Hallowed be your name": In the ancient world, to name something was to acknowledge and participate in its presence. In this part of the prayer, we participate in God's presence among us as "Father."

"Your kingdom come": These words continue the blessing, as we ask to know the presence of God's kingdom, not somebody else's. Consciously or unconsciously, willingly or unwillingly, we are part of various realms: family, workplace or career, community, country, and world. In this petition we declare our primary residence in God's kingdom.

"Your will be done": Similarly, we ask for God's will to be done, not somebody else's—or our own. God does not will suffering. God's will is for God's creatures to flourish! This petition invites us to "let go—and let God."

"Give us this day our daily bread": Here is a series of petitions for the three basic things we need for the journey of discipleship: food, forgiveness, and freedom from temptation. In ancient Palestine, life depended on a good harvest and enough rain. Doubly taxed by military and temple hierarchies, people scrambled for enough to eat. At the same time, the petition reminds us of the source of all good things: God, the Giver of every gift.

"Forgive us our sins as we forgive those who sin against us": Forgiveness ranks alongside our need for food and for protection from temptation as something essential to Christian discipleship. Why? Without forgiveness we as disciples would travel alone, alienated from others by slights and petty grievances. These words chart a course of reconciliation for every disciple. And even as we ask for forgiveness, we are reminded that we need to forgive.

"Save us from the time of trial and deliver us from evil": Stop to think of all the ways in which we are "possessed" today—by the pursuit of possessions, success, status, and more. Jesus invites us to pray for deliverance from all these things.

Did You Know?

• Orthodox Christians have a familiar prayer that they use as a kind of mantra—the *Trisagion*, meaning "three-times blessed." It blesses God in three ways: "Holy God, holy and mighty, holy and immortal: have mercy on us."

Food, forgiveness, and freedom from temptation are three things disciples need, like the air we breathe. But we are also invited to pray for what we need. God promises that our prayers will be answered. They may not be answered in the ways we expect or in the ways we want. But God answers them. Prayer keeps us open for God's answers—sometimes answers to questions we didn't even know we had.

"For the kingdom, the power, and the glory are yours, now and forever": The prayer concludes as it began, with reference to God's kingdom, blessing the only kingdom that counts.

"Amen": In Luke's account of the Lord's Prayer, God's blessings spill over the lip of discipleship and onto a thirsty world. Jesus continues his prayer with three very concrete examples of this: feeding those who are hungry, welcoming the stranger, and honoring the friend. These are not just metaphors to show us our dependence on God; nor are they examples to show us how to ask God for everything. They are Jesus' Amen to the prayer. Offer food, hospitality, and honor to all those in need of these things.

 What are some ways you could remind yourself to think about the words you're saying when you pray the Lord's Prayer?

Naming the Baby

Drawing upon all the rich imagery of the Hebrew scriptures, medieval monks developed a particular rite of welcoming and naming as they prepared for the birth of Christ. From December 17 through 23, they offered special prayers naming the God they anticipated in the Christ-child: Wisdom from on high, Lord of Might, Root of Jesse, Key of David, Dayspring from on high, Ruler of all nations, and God with us.

Using the first letter of each of these titles in Latin and reversing the sequence spells out the Latin phrase *ero cras*, which means "Tomorrow I will be with you!"

What are some ways you could name God in your prayers? What names have you heard for God—in the Bible or in hymns and songs, for example? Try to come up with a name for God that you haven't used or heard before.

Forgive Us as We Forgive Others: Roberta Bondi

Roberta Bondi, a contemporary scholar, theologian, and spiritual writer, says the Lord's Prayer changed her life.

Bondi was on the faculty of a large, prestigious university. One of her colleagues—who was also a friend—betrayed her, damaging her deeply. Bondi agonized for days, weighing how to respond, struggling not to retaliate. She found an answer in the Lord's Prayer.

Initially, she did not want to see her colleague as a child of God, but praying to "*our* Father" meant she couldn't consider her colleague only as an adversary, but also as her sister in Christ. To ease her anger, Bondi deliberately prayed to "our Father, that is, *my* Father and the Father of. . . ."

Over time, the prayer made way for a reconciliation that Bondi could not have reached on her own. She never completely relinquished her guard with this colleague, and the friendship was never on the same footing again. But Bondi forgave her colleague and saw her as a child of God.

Wrap-up

The Lord's Prayer teaches us how to pray, what to pray for, and where God wants us to serve. The Amen turns us toward our neighbors to give food, hospitality, and honor.

In the next faith practice, study, we look critically at God's word and the world, asking where the two intersect.

PS Take time with God. Make time with God. Just show up.

In My Life

- Pray the Lord's Prayer every day this week—slowly enough to think about the words you're saying.
- Make a commitment to pray and live out the Amen by offering food, hospitality, and honor to those who need these things.
- Listen for all the ways God is named the next time you are at worship. Make a mental list.
- Pick a psalm—any psalm—and notice how is God named.
- Pray the Jesus Prayer throughout one day.

BIBLE 6

How do I discover more about the Bible?

Bible Study

Key Text: Luke 10:29-37
Key Idea: In the practice of study, God speaks to us through the Bible today.

BIBLE 7

Step-by-step: Bible Study

Preparation: Set up a time and place to meet.
Contact group members.
Tools and materials: Bibles
Time: approximately 60 minutes

1 Gather and read a Bible text together. Read it silently. Take time for meditation if you wish. Then read the text aloud. (Be creative. You can use several different readers, role-play, read antiphonally, and so forth.)

2 Discuss: What is God doing in this text? What is God saying to us today, through this text?

3 Take time for further study.

4 Share what you've learned with others.

 Expect surprises! God speaks to us through the Bible. You might hear something new, even if a text is very familiar to you.

 What are some benefits of studying the Bible with others?

Listen

The Bible is God's word. That means God speaks through the Bible—speaks to us. Two basic questions can help us listen to what God is saying to us through the Bible today.

1. What is God doing in this text?

Listen to what happens in the Bible passage. Who is in it, and what are they doing? Where is God? What is God saying? What is God doing?

It can be helpful—and fascinating—to get more information on what was happening in the world at the time the text was written, what is happening in the text itself, and what the writer was trying to do. Bible study guides and other resources designed for the group study of scripture often gather this kind of information for you, but you can check study Bibles, Bible commentaries, and history resources at home, in a church library or public library, or even online. For example, Jesus' parable of the Good Samaritan (Luke 10:29-37) is the text for this lesson on faith practices. If it was the text for a Bible study, you and your group could learn about people in the first and second century, their social, religious, economic, and political dynamics; their views on race, gender, and class; and—especially important for this parable—the relationship between Jews and Samaritans. You could look at the audience (the first readers or hearers of these words), the writer's purpose, and the text itself as a literary unit.

2. What is God saying to us today, through this text?

Listen for what God is saying through the text. What do you hear? What is God saying to you, to your group, to your congregation, and so on?

At this point, it can be helpful to have a good awareness of what is happening in the world right now. With the parable of the Good Samaritan, your study could include some tough questions: What is our world like? What does this text mean for us today? Are there situations today similar to the one between Jews and Samaritans? If so, what are they? Who are the Samaritans in our community? Who is lying by the side of the road? Who are the priests and Levites in our community? Where do we see compassion? How might we "go and do likewise"?

 What kind of Bible study resources are readily available to your group? Why is listening such a big part of Bible study?

A Life of Study

Martin Luther not only considered "study" a faith practice and one of the "marks of the church," he lived it out. His study of scripture led him to teach on the theological faculty at the

University of Wittenberg; write numerous biblical commentaries, including important works on Genesis, Isaiah, Galatians, and the Psalms; and translate the Bible into the language of the people. As pastor, preacher, and theologian, he drew from scripture to address questions and issues in sixteenth-century Germany.

 In what ways will you live out the practice of Bible study?

Listening to God: A Bible Study Group

A group of friends from the congregation started meeting at a local restaurant at 6:00 A.M. Tuesday mornings for Bible study. Their schedules were full of activities with family, friends, work, and church. Still, each person made time to show up every Tuesday.

Each meeting started with someone reading a scripture passage out loud, right there in the restaurant. While they waited for their orders, the friends talked about the text and what was happening in it. By the time they were ready to move the discussion on to something else, breakfast had usually arrived. As they ate, they talked about what God was saying today through the Bible text. That had seemed strange at first, but, as time went on, that changed. They had always enjoyed talking to each other, but now they were listening too—and listening to God.

 What opportunities are available to you for Bible study with a group? If you started a new group for people not already involved in Bible study, what time would it meet? Where would it meet?

Wrap-up

The practice of Bible study encourages us to read the Bible and listen for God speaking to us.

In the next faith practice, we hear God speaking to us through the Bible as we gather with others in worship.

 Mark your calendar and make time. Put Bible study group sessions on your calendar with other meetings and commitments.

In My Life

- Find out about Bible study opportunities by checking a worship bulletin or church newsletter or talking with a pastor. If there isn't an opportunity at a time and place that works for you, find a few friends and start your own group.
- If you are in a Bible study group already, invite someone to come with you to the next session.
- If you are new to Bible study, look for a group that plans to meet for a certain period of time (over the summer, or during Advent or Lent, for instance). This is a good way to get started with study.

How do I discover more about the Bible?

Hearing God's Word in Worship

Key Text: Psalm 95:6
Key Idea: In hearing God's word in worship, we gather and listen to God's word read and preached, we taste God's word, and, fed by God's word, we scatter to serve.

Step-by-step: Worship

1

Gather to worship.

2

Hear the word. Listen to the word of God as it is read from scripture and preached from the pulpit.

3 Taste the word. Having heard the word, share in the body and blood of Christ.

4 Scatter to serve, fed by God's word.

DIY You might find it helpful to follow along in a Bible as the word is read. Some congregations provide Bibles in the pew for you to use, or you can bring a Bible with you to worship.

? *We can hear and taste God's word in worship. How often do you think you need to do this?*

Active Listening

Hearing God's word in worship does not involve passive listening, but a complex series of calls and responses. The first scripture reading calls out to us and, in many congregations, we respond with one of the psalms. The second reading calls out to us and we respond with "Alleluia." The Gospel reading calls out to us and we respond by acknowledging it as the word of God: "Praise to you, O Christ."

The sermon responds to the Gospel, offering an interpretation of what scripture means in the world today. The hymn following the sermon also responds to the Gospel. It proclaims the word of God in song. The Apostles' Creed follows as an outburst of faith, using words that other believers, living and dead, have used and uniting us with their confession. The prayers of the church bring the congregation together in praise, petition, and blessing. Finally, we celebrate the unity that God has worked in our midst by sharing the peace. All of these elements comprise what is known as the "Office of the Word."

Active listening in worship continues with communion. We hear the words inviting us to this meal and we take part in it. We are fed with the body and blood of Christ, who is

God's Word. This food nurtures us to go out into the world to serve.

 Are you a good listener? How could you listen more effectively when God's word is read, preached, and offered in communion?

Listen Up

We can't hear the word of God unless we listen. And we can't listen if there is a lot of background noise—distractions, worries, grudges, and so forth. The more we have on our minds, the longer it takes to clear our minds and be able to listen to God. Hearing the word requires space for listening.

Along with space for listening, hearing the word requires attention. Martin Luther wished that he could attend to the holy word of God the way his dog sat under the dinner table waiting for a bone. Every muscle strains for the smallest morsel—that's the way to be attentive to the word.

The Old Testament uses the word "hearken" to captures this quality of attention. There is a mutual "hearkening" between God and God's people, as one party calls upon the

Did You Know?

• Many congregations provide hearing aids for worship. Some also provide a sign language interpreter. If you have a hearing impairment, contact the church office or an usher to find out what is available.

other. Listen to the words of the great Hebrew prayer, the Shema: "Hear, O Israel: The LORD is our God, the LORD alone" (Deuteronomy 6:4). The language is elegant, but the meaning is blunt: "Listen up!" "Why aren't you paying attention to me?"

What are some ways to clear your mind of background noise before and during worship?

An Active Listener: Christina

Christina took her seat in the church choir, just minutes before the Easter worship service was about to start. This was the third and last service of the day—the choir had already sung at the sunrise service and the early service. Now Christina realized she couldn't remember anything from the scripture readings or the sermon from the earlier two services. She decided to make the most of this final opportunity.

Christina listened for God's word, from the start of worship through the scripture readings, sermon, and communion. She heard that Jesus conquered death and sin, and is alive and active in our lives and in the world. She was fed by the bread and wine.

At the end of worship, when the pastor said, "Go in peace. Serve the Lord!" Christina was ready. "Thanks be to God!" she answered.

Wrap-up

In the practice of hearing God's word in worship, God speaks to us through the Bible.

The faith practices in this unit explore discipleship and focus on the Bible. In the next unit, we continue to explore discipleship with faith practices that focus on God.

 PS Everyone's mind wanders sometimes. If you are distracted from listening for God's word in worship, focus again on the sights, sounds, and tastes in the service.

In My Life

- Find out what scripture texts will be used at the next weekly worship service. Read and meditate on these texts in advance. Then attend worship and listen actively.
- Volunteer to be a lector in your congregation, if possible.
- Keep in mind that God speaks to us through the Bible still today.
- Read scripture passages to an elderly person. If the person has some favorite passages, read those. If not, read some of your favorites or choose a psalm that fits the situation.

BIBLE 8

God 1
How do I experience God?

Centering Prayer

Key Text: Psalm 141:1-2
Key Idea: The deliberate, meditative, peaceful practice of centering prayer renews us and our relationship with God.

GOD 1

Step-by-Step: Centering Prayer

Preparation: Find a regular time and a regular place to really focus on you and on God.

Tools and materials: Select a candle, fountain, painting, or picture to use as a focal point during prayer. Peaceful music, or even just background static, can be helpful. Have something to read—a Bible marked with a few key verses, a favorite devotional, or a hymnal.

Time: 15 minutes a week, or more if possible

1 Begin with quiet prayer, focusing on your conversation with God.

2 Read a few select passages at a time. Pause frequently to meditate on what these words mean for you and your time with God.

Close with a brief spoken prayer (perhaps the Lord's Prayer or Psalm 23).

 If you find your attention drifting, change it up a bit. Switch positions, verses, postures—whatever focuses you.

How does this kind of prayer differ from your typical prayer style? Could you make it your regular prayer practice? Why or why not?

God's Word—Your Center

For a lot of Christians prayer comes at only two times: at the dinner table, or when you shout out a quick "Help!" in God's direction. Like any kind of relationship, however, there needs to be regular communication between you and God. Centering prayer makes your time with God intentional and focused, allowing you to have meaningful conversation.

Prayer has been seen as a kind of sacrifice to God, and when you consider how hard it can be to "sacrifice" personal time to pray, this makes sense. The verse "Let my prayer be counted as incense before you, and the lifting up of my hands as an evening sacrifice" (Psalm 141:2) refers back to sacrificial practices. Incense was one kind of sacrifice to be offered to God. The psalmist is asking that prayers, both in words and physical action, be like incense or sacrifices to God.

Rushing around without giving time to prayer denies you a special time with God, and denies God the time and space God wants with you. When you don't spend time in prayer with God, it's like you aren't recognizing the importance of God in your life.

Throughout the Bible, we see people going off alone for focused, life-giving prayer. Moses, David, and Peter all find it important to their ministry, and Jesus

Did You Know?

• According to Exodus 30, incense had to be offered daily to God in the holiest part of the temple. Each ingredient was specified and laid out exactly—it was (and still is!) a very important ceremony!

GOD 1

84

frequently leaves the crowds (and even his disciples) behind to talk to his Father. These prayers came at times of great need and distress along with times of conversation with God and renewal of the relationship.

Through centering prayer, you focus your mind on God's grace. This reminder of God's love and providence needs to come every day, not just when you think you need it. Christian faith has always placed importance on a healthy prayer life for this reason. Peaceful, centering prayer reminds us who we are and keeps our experience of God's simple, profound gifts fresh in our life. While the time feels like a sacrifice, it is well worth it.

 In what ways can prayer be a sacrifice? Why do you think even the most holy of biblical figures needed to offer that sacrifice as well?

A Center Point for Faith

There are many different forms of prayer: group (or corporate) prayer, prayer in music, labyrinth prayer, and many more. The form changes based on the kind of prayer being offered and the reason for the prayer. For example, a prayer on behalf of a community for safety might be offered in corporate prayer, while personal prayers for guidance and wisdom might find voice in music.

Centering prayer can find some of its roots in the ancient practice of *lectio divina* (Latin for divine reading). *Lectio divina* has four steps: read a Bible passage thoroughly, reflect on the passage, open your heart to God for conversation, and listen for God's response. This process has been around for more than 1600 years and is often considered one of the most interactive, prayerful ways to read scripture. Since it also requires stillness and meditative prayer, *lectio divina* lends itself well to regular prayer practice as well as Bible study. Eventually *lectio divina* became a separate movement of its own.

Centering prayer also draws insight from ancient prayer practices of the Christian contemplative heritage, from men and women who spent time in solitary desert life. These hermits would deliberately go out in the wilderness to spend time alone with God, reflecting on God's nature and praying for wisdom and insight. This sort of prayer style, frequently associated with monastic life, lost favor around the time of the Reformation, along with many monastic practices.

More recently, interest in centering prayer has been renewed as a peaceful, God-centered way to return to conversation with God in a slower, more restorative way. Since it requires a passionate, solitary conversation with God, it runs against what many people think prayer can be—fast, easy, and cheap. Today, people and churches across denominations turn to centering prayer to renew and revive faith life and prayer practice.

 How does the history of centering prayer influence your participation in it? What insight for your prayer life can it give you?

Practicing One Man's Passion

In southern France, a group of non-denominational Christians gather together in Taizé. Their life together consists of praying together three times a day plus living frugally and responsibly. Brother Roger founded the community together with others on Easter Day of 1949, after World War II. A peaceful, contemplative man, he wanted others to have time and space to experience the deep, gracious love of God in community.

This faith community has spread its style of worship and prayer worldwide. Especially important to Taizé prayer is song, which focuses the mind and unifies people. Also, silence, scripture, and brief prayers are integrated into the services. Icons (images of Jesus and saints) and candlelight serve to center and focus those at prayer.

While the primary members of the Taizé remain on-site, others are always welcome to join them. Also, the practices of the community transfer easily to corporate or personal worship, as they simply encourage people to spend time in worshipful prayer with God. Songs, icons, candles, and a program might help, but the intent of the prayer can be followed by anyone.

Wrap-up

In the practice of centering prayer, we move into conversation with God. The next practice, silence, focuses on the listening side of that conversation.

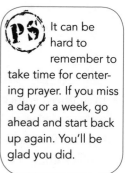

It can be hard to remember to take time for centering prayer. If you miss a day or a week, go ahead and start back up again. You'll be glad you did.

In My Life

- Schedule time every week to dedicate to prayer. Make sure you are awake, focused, and calm.
- Combine centering prayer with your regular scripture reading so you can pray and study your way through the Bible.
- Try different objects, readings, or places to focus your prayer.
- Mark important passages whenever you read your Bible, especially verses that might give you hope or support for particular situations. When you are ready to pray, these verses will be ready for you to read and focus on.
- Sing, chant, dance, or otherwise change up your centering prayer. The point is to keep your attention on God and your conversation, so anything that serves that purpose and enhances your prayer life works.
- Consider incorporating a practice from the Taizé community into your personal prayer life.

GOD 1

How do I experience God?

Silence

Key Text: Lamentations 3:24-28
Key Idea: Silence not only quiets the mind and calms the body, but it allows for time and space to focus on and listen to God.

Step-by-step: Silence

Preparation: Pick a time and place where you can regularly be in silence – both outside yourself and inside yourself.
Tools and materials: Have a journal, sketch book, or something else available to describe your experience and thoughts.
Time: 30 minutes each week

1 Prepare. Get your chosen space ready—phone off, door closed. Find a comfortable posture. Set a period of time for silence and hold yourself to it.

2 Take a deep breath, calm your thoughts, and listen carefully for any ideas, thoughts, questions, or suggestions that come to you. Consider how God might be speaking to you through them. Try journaling, drawing, or whatever you choose to relate and express your time.

3 Close with a brief prayer, saying thanks for God's presence with you.

 Don't hesitate to use earplugs! Sometimes you can't control the surrounding sounds, so feel free to block them out.

 What is the value of silence? Why is it so hard to maintain? How do you think silent time can help you experience God in your life?

GOD 2

The Gift of Silence

We might turn to God and demand, "Why aren't you answering me?" but we might just as well ask ourselves why we aren't listening for God. Life is full of distractions, many of which simply cannot be avoided. It's easy to get caught up in all the noise and frenzy. Sometimes things get so noisy for so long that we forget to start listening again. When we're surrounded with sound, we start to add to the problem and try to yell over the fray, making it even harder to find peace.

When you're trying to shout over the noise in your life, which is drowning out God's word, a few things happen. First of all, you will probably say things you will regret later. Next, you never get a chance to recover from the chaos and reflect on what is happening in your life. Most importantly, you never get a chance to talk to God, much less hear what God is saying to you.

In the key verse for this lesson, the author of Lamentations is doing just what the title of the book suggests: lamenting. In the midst of all his suffering, anxiety, fear, and frustration, he recalls that there have indeed been times when God was merciful and helpful. He knows that all things come from God and that God is worth the wait. So he decides that instead of continuing to yell and hope his curses are heard over the noise, he stops, closes his mouth, sits quietly, and listens for God's wisdom. He begins to realize that God was listening all along. He was the one who couldn't hear God.

Silence has great value in the Bible. It can be a sort of punishment, forcing someone to stop talking when everything they say is full of doubt, accusation, and anger. However, silence also allows people time and space to grieve, find the right words for worship, listen to God's answers for prayers offered, focus in on right teaching, and better understand what is going on in daily life. Silence is a gift, if you can learn to accept it. In the silence, we can finally hear the still, peaceful voice of God granting guidance and answering prayer.

Did You Know?

• Silence is technically defined as 20 decibels, which is roughly the same as leaves rustling or a mosquito buzzing. This is quieter than a whisper. On average, a person deals with 76 decibels throughout the day— about the level of city traffic or a hair dryer.

Have you ever had a time when it was hard to stay silent? What about a time when silence was all you needed to hear?

The Silent Witness

Silence has found great support, especially within monastic circles. Long trained to find ways to worship and pray outside of the norm, monastics have practiced silence both as self-discipline and religious endeavor. Their practice and witness

GOD 2

have taught many others about silence and the way it can help people connect with God's word for them.

St. Benedict lived and worked in Italy during the sixth century. He wrote a guide that is referred to as "The Rule of St. Benedict." In this little book he outlined beliefs and ways of life—everything from the different kinds of monks that can exist to the appropriate forms of punishment for breaking community rules. While some of the book is more relevant to earlier times, a lot of it still helps guide both monastics and lay people even today.

St. Benedict wrote a whole chapter in his book on the importance of silence for religious life. He believed that silence was truly central to devoted, centered lives of faith. Silence allows time for prayer and reflection and promotes listening, which allows learning. He advocated an active life balanced with specific times and places where silence would be more strictly adhered to, making silence as much a part of life as anything else.

Today, different monastic orders hold to the rules of silence in different ways. Some are strict about imposing silence, even creating a series of signs so that brothers and sisters adhering to silence can still interact with other people while not breaking their promise. Others are lenient, seeing silence as something to be undertaken for shorter periods of time and for more specific purposes. No matter what, these devotees see silence as a blessing to overcome self and the world and to communicate more deeply with God.

 How can periods of silence help order your life? Do you think it would be easier or harder to be in a community where silence was imposed? Can you make silence part of the "rule" for your own life?

A Much-Needed Retreat

For a week, a group of camp counselors in training had been meeting each other, learning rules, practicing Bible studies, teaching songs, and basically wearing themselves down. Many staff members were already coming down with colds and looking bleary-eyed, and there was still another week of training to go. At this rate, this group was going to burn themselves out before the campers even arrived.

Exhausted herself, the camp director declared a day of silence at morning worship. No one was allowed to talk all day, no matter what. She suggested that the counselors spend the time in reflection and prayer, but if what they really needed was a hike or a nap, that was all right too. At first, the counselors were dismayed—how could they get to know each other if they couldn't talk?

But after just a few minutes, they started to get the idea. Some sat on the beach, others took time to explore the camp, and others read the Bible, while some chose to sit in the trees and meditate. No matter what they did, they found their energy returning. They remembered why they wanted to do camp ministry in the first place. They found they had rediscovered their sense of self, their call to service, and their love for each other. At breakfast the next morning, when speech was reinstated, they were more able to share themselves and enjoy each other. The time spent free of noise and chatter had provided them a chance to hear what God had to say to each and every person.

Wrap-up

In the practice of silence, we listen for God and the ways God is working in our lives. The next practice, gratitude, focuses on giving thanks for God's actions and responses to our prayers.

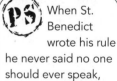

When St. Benedict wrote his rule he never said no one should ever speak, only that we probably speak more than we should and often without listening.

In My Life

- Choose a time when your silence won't be a problem for yourself, your family, or your work.
- Consider making short periods of "alone time" a regular practice for your household, so that you can all benefit from a little peace and quiet.
- Reflect regularly on the kinds of journaling you do during your silent times. Can you see any patterns or trends developing?
- Bring a group of friends, family members, or coworkers together in a silent retreat. Go camping or spend time at a retreat center where you can all be together in silence and discuss the experience at the end.
- Consider taking a silent retreat once a month along with or instead of practicing silence weekly. Spend a whole day or weekend in contemplative silence.
- Take time for silence when you find yourself run down, exhausted, confused, or overworked. Fill up with God's love and grace.

God 3

How do I experience God?

Gratitude

Key Text: Colossians 3:16-17
Key Idea: The practice of gratitude expresses our faith to God, who provides for us no matter what.

GOD 3

Step-by-Step: Gratitude

Preparation: Choose a journal for recording your prayer requests and responses—a notebook or book that can include a collage of magazine clippings, photos, or sketches.
Tools and materials: your prayer journal
Time: 15 minutes daily or weekly

1 Note the things that you are asking God for. Try to be as specific as possible.

2 Pray. Talk with God about these things that are in your heart.

3 Look back regularly at past entries and think about how God has been at work in those things.

4 When you see ways God has responded to your prayers, note them in your journal. Pray and give thanks to God.

DIY When you set up your journal, consider using two columns or facing pages for each entry. Use one side for the prayer and the other side for responses. Include dates with each entry too.

? *What does it really mean for you to show gratitude to God? How can a prayer journal encourage you to be more thankful?*

Gracious Gratitude

Maybe you remember writing out a thank-you note to a relative for a sweater you weren't really sure you wanted. It was awkward, forced, and not particularly grateful. Sometimes saying thank you can feel like a chore, especially when what you got wasn't exactly what you asked for. A lot of the time, it's just easier to ask for something else rather than be thankful for what you have been given.

Our faith tells us that everything we have comes from God. God created an amazing world for us to live in and took care of every detail—from food, air, and water to music, friends, and chocolate. Intuitively, we all know that God's graciousness is indeed the source of all these amazing things. Realistically, we take all this for granted and forget how God constantly works in our lives. Instead of taking time in our lives to thank God for what we've already been given, we spend more time wishing that we had even more. It's easy to get caught up in the things we don't have, all the while forgetting to thank God for what we do have.

In the book of Colossians, Paul is encouraging the people of Colossae, a community he has never seen, to remain faithful to Christ and the teachings of the church. Paul's passionate desire is for them to live fully in God's grace. He lays out for them a way of life that not only reflects God's love in their world, but also enacts it for other people. Along with a list of other traits, Paul includes gratitude. He wants the Colossians to have a thankfulness that overflows into song and praise, not just an obligatory throw-away note.

Paul knew that in order to really understand the relationship they had with God, the Colossians had to be thankful. Not only that, they had to live out that gratitude. In fact, this gratitude was not limited to responses to the good things God had done. These thanks were to be given in everything they did, either in word or deed, in the name of Christ. This is an embodied gratitude, one where the incredible things God has done are talked about, lived out, and even sung about!

This is the kind of gratitude God wants from us. It's not just a quick mention in passing. It's a way of life that recognizes God as the gracious center of all things.

What does it mean to live a life of gratitude? If you were to write a thank-you note to God, what kind of things would you include? How would you explain your thanks to other people?

Taking Notes on God

In a big way, Paul's epistles are his prayer journals. Granted, he intended them as letters to congregations for instruction and support. However, today we can look back at his writings and consider the ways God worked in the early church. Paul's prayers, concerns, requests, and celebrations inspire us in our faith and remind us of the ways that God works in our lives even today.

People of faith throughout the centuries have been journaling their thoughts and prayers. While we have access to these journals today, many were never intended to be read by anyone else. They were ways for people of faith to maintain focus and strength when times were tough, and gratitude and celebration when times were good. Journaling prayer requests and responses is such a natural practice that it never really got started by anyone in particular—it's simply a wise, helpful way to experience God in daily life.

Did You Know?

• A prayer journal can be started by anyone of any age at any time.

Because life has gotten faster and more complicated, we are in more need than ever of the kind of good work God does in our lives. Prayer journals are enjoying a revival as more and more people discover how a prayer journal keeps one focused on God and truly grateful for the new and incredible ways that God works. Not only can we be inspired by the words of people of faith from ages past, but we can continue to be inspired by God's action here and now.

 If someone were to read your prayer journal centuries from now, what kind of testimony would you hope it would leave? How could your faith be lived out in gratitude?

Grateful, Not Anxious

Becky is a mother of three adult children spread out across the country. She does her best to stay in touch with them all, but sometimes the distance between them overwhelms her. Whenever she prays for her children, she finds herself getting caught up with all her fears and frustrations and rarely thanking God for keeping them happy, safe, and healthy. Sometimes, it's hard for her to even believe that God listens to her anymore.

At her Bible study group, people got talking about prayer journals. One woman told about how relieved she was when she could look back and see that God was indeed working in her life. Becky was so interested that her friend even let her take a look at her prayer journal, which she carries with her everywhere. Becky was impressed to see that her friend even wrote down answers to prayers that she didn't want to see but was thankful for anyway.

Now when she sits down to pray, Becky keeps her prayer journal with her. She is constantly amazed to see how, in spite of her anxieties, God remains active in her family's life. She feels freer to be truly grateful for God's guidance and even more appreciative of the diverse interests of her kids. Becky's prayer journal keeps her centered in gratitude instead of pulled apart by her fears.

Wrap-up

In the practice of gratitude, we give thanks for God's actions in our lives and responses to our prayers. The next practice, Sabbath-keeping, focuses on pausing to give thanks and celebrate God's graciousness in our lives.

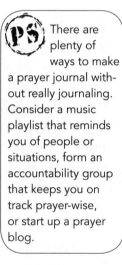

PS There are plenty of ways to make a prayer journal without really journaling. Consider a music playlist that reminds you of people or situations, form an accountability group that keeps you on track prayer-wise, or start up a prayer blog.

In My Life

- Make your prayer journal portable so you can jot things down as you think of them.
- Schedule a time and place for daily or weekly journaling.
- Try combining styles (writing, collage, music) for a more dynamic journal.
- Consider sharing your journal with someone, maybe even someone you've been praying for, as a way to share your thanks.

God 4

How do I experience God?

Sabbath-Keeping

Key Text: Isaiah 58:13-14

Key Idea: Keeping Sabbath means pausing to celebrate God's graciousness and give thanks for things we might otherwise take for granted.

GOD 4

Step-by-Step: Sabbath-Keeping

While the traditional Christian practice is to spend all day on Sunday in Sabbath, sometimes that's not possible. However, it's still vital for you and your faith to spend a substantial piece of your week in Sabbath time.

Preparation: Have the worship schedule for your congregation available.
Tools and materials: your schedule or calendar
Time: one day a week (If that's absolutely not possible, at least set aside time for prayer and praise.)

1 Set aside time. Plan ahead. Make sure your schedule is really and truly clear for your Sabbath time.

2 Start with worship. Allow it to be the center of your day and your week.

3

Celebrate a day of rest and rejuvenation with the loved ones in your life.

 Do whatever it takes to keep this time holy. Don't be ashamed to turn down meetings or work if they would prevent your Sabbath time!

4

End the day with worship or prayer as a reminder that the Sabbath is from God, for you.

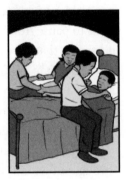

Why is it so hard to take time out of your schedule for Sabbath time? What's the difference between being lazy and observing the Sabbath? What do you think are the benefits to regular Sabbath-keeping?

The Sabbath Was Made for Us

The original biblical model of Sabbath-keeping begins in Genesis 2:2: "And on the seventh day God finished the work that he had done, and he rested on the seventh day from all the work that he had done." A better translation of "rested" would actually be "ceased," since God doesn't need to stop working yet chose to pause for that day. God marked the seventh day as a time to step back, admire the good things in the world, and be blessed. The Sabbath is one day of the week for us to pause from our work and appreciate all the incredible things that have been made and done for us. No "work" should be done on the Sabbath, since it would be a distraction from our time of thanks and praise to God. Instead, the Sabbath is a time to relax, worship, pray, and celebrate.

Since God instituted the Sabbath, God's people had to try to figure out exactly what was the best way to observe it. Throughout Exodus and Leviticus you can read about the Israelites trying to determine what things could and should be done on the Sabbath. In fact, as one of the Ten Commandments, the Sabbath became so important that not observing it could result in death by stoning!

Eventually, people were splitting hairs about what exactly constituted "work" and who was doing a better job of not working than others. The initial, life-giving intention of a day of rest and worship got twisted into legalism. This is why Jesus says in Mark 2:27, "The sabbath was made for humankind, and not humankind for the sabbath." God did not intend the Sabbath to be another rule to follow, but to be an opportunity for us to cease from our work and remind ourselves of God's creation, every detail.

The writer of Isaiah holds this same intent. (Read the key Bible text, Isaiah 58:13-14.) God means for you to enjoy the Sabbath. If you make it into a rule that makes you sound more pious, you're misusing it just as much as people who decide not to observe a day of rest. The Bible tells us clearly that God gave us the gift of Sabbath to rest, refocus, refuel, and really focus on worship and praise. How can you argue with that?

• Modern Jews categorize 39 different categories of activities as *melachah*, or work, that cannot be done on the Sabbath. These things all relate to creative activities, mirroring God's rest after six days of creation.

How does the biblical model of Sabbath-keeping affect your observance of the Sabbath? What does this set-aside time mean for the way you structure work, play, worship, and life?

The People of the Sabbath

Initially, the ancient Jews kept the Sabbath from sundown on Friday to sundown on Saturday. When the first Christians started practicing the Sabbath, they did the same thing. However, within a few hundred years, Christians started having their day of rest and worship on Sunday. There may have been many reasons for this, including attempts to distinguish Christianity from Judaism and to replace other pagan worship days held on Sunday.

The pattern for Sabbath-keeping on Sundays included worship with the community, large meals with friends and family, and a day off from work done during the rest of the week. In many ways, this pattern exists up until today, where Jews and Christians of many denominations use the Sabbath day as a time for worship, family, relaxation, and rest.

Some people have placed great emphasis on the Sabbath as a requirement for salvation. In this line of thought, if people observe the Sabbath rightly and on the correct day, they are not only true believers but might even instigate the return of Christ to the world. As attractive as this is, it is not the intent of Sabbath. Sabbath observance isn't just another rule to be followed. Christ himself said that the Sabbath was made for us and not the other way around.

Recently, the concept of Sabbath as more than just one day of the week has emerged. This stems from the fact that fewer and fewer people actually take the time to observe any kind of Sabbath day. Modern society makes it difficult to have a day of rest when businesses are open seven days a week and employees might work at any hour of the week. Instead of designating just one day a week as Sabbath, more people have come to understand Sabbath as any period designated for rest and worship.

More and more churches offer worship services outside of Sunday morning. Not only does this accommodate different schedules, it embodies the fact that Sabbath is important no matter what day of the week it is. After all, God intended the Sabbath to be a time for believers to step back and remember who they are and whose they are. Sabbath time is holy time, meant to give the believer time and space outside of day-to-day life.

Did You Know?

• One reason given for observing the Christian Sabbath on Sunday is the concept of the "eighth day." Since Christ was raised on Sunday, it marks a day of new creation and new Sabbath following the seventh day (Saturday) when God paused from creation.

 Do you think the Sabbath should be on one day or another? Why or why not? How would you observe the Sabbath if you couldn't take a Sunday off?

A Modern Sabbath

Keeping the Sabbath day holy is extremely important in Judaism even today. Traditionally, work such as cooking, gardening, and even walking was considered work prohibited on the Sabbath.

Some contemporary Jews, however, think these activities are exactly the kinds of things that should happen on a day of rest and celebration. They believe that things people find relaxing and celebratory should not be prohibited on the Sabbath. They leave it up to each individual believer to decide how to appropriately observe the Sabbath. In this line of thinking, the Sabbath should not be an opportunity for guilt and condemnation but for personal and corporate celebration.

Wrap-up

In the practice of Sabbath-keeping, we pause to give thanks and celebrate God's graciousness in our lives. The next practices, baptism and communion, were instituted by Christ himself and are the most powerful ways for us to experience his presence together as a community.

 We don't exactly live in a Sabbath-friendly world. Sometimes our holidays are even more work than workdays! Remind yourself that Sabbath time is for you to keep your relationship with God strong and healthy.

In My Life

- Plan your week around your Sabbath. Take care of work ahead of time to keep your Sabbath uninterrupted.
- Consider different ways to enhance Sabbath time. Trips to see family members, a visit to a museum, or a day hike are all great ideas.
- Involve others in your Sabbath-keeping. They keep you accountable, and Sabbath means more when celebrated with others.
- Try to take your Sabbath on a day when you can be at church or involved in some kind of corporate worship. The Sabbath is about God, after all!

God 5

How do I experience God?

Baptism and Communion

Key Text: Titus 3:4-7

Key Idea: Baptism and communion, instituted by Christ himself, are the most powerful ways for us to experience his presence together as a community.

GOD 5

Step-by-step: Baptism and Communion

You are not meant to celebrate baptism and communion by yourself, yet these steps can help you appreciate these sacraments more fully.

Preparation: Try to find out ahead of time if there will be communion and/or a baptism at worship.
Tools and materials: A worship bulletin and hymnal to follow along through the service
Time: the duration of a worship service

1

Spend some time in prayer to prepare.

> **DIY** Consider obtaining a copy of a baptismal and/or communion service to take home. Feel free to study it or even memorize it. Not only can it help you be more engaged during worship, it can be very encouraging outside of worship.

2 Really watch and listen for God's promises during a baptism or communion. What does it mean for you to be claimed as God's child? What does it mean to you that the bread and wine hold Christ's promise to be present?

3 Participate actively. Think about the congregational responses as you say them. Welcome a new sister or brother in Christ. Receive the body and blood of Christ, given for you.

 Do you usually take communion for granted? Do you feel frustrated when a baptism takes up more worship time? How can you be fully present in these experiences during worship?

This Is for You!

Jesus' baptism comes early on in three of the Gospels—Matthew 3, Luke 3, and John 1. And, yes, you read that correctly: Jesus himself was baptized. If nothing else, this is evidence that baptism doesn't make you any more holy (since Christ was the Son of God already), but is nonetheless very important for a life of faith. And so we are baptized because Jesus was baptized, and he called his followers to make disciples and baptize.

Jesus also instituted the meal that we celebrate in communion. Matthew 26, Mark 14, Luke 24, and John 13 all tell the story of the meal Christ shared with his disciples, in which he promised that whenever we drink the wine and eat the bread, he is with us. He even promises that through this meal we receive forgiveness from sins. Communion is more than symbols or ideas. It is the real deal.

We don't participate in baptism or communion because these things make us godly, or because we have to or we're in trouble, or because we will be better than others. We participate because we want to. In the sacraments of baptism and communion, we are claimed as children of God and fed and cared for accordingly. In these sacraments, we really and truly experience God first-hand.

Here's the thing: there's no magic "hocus pocus" going on, but there's still something very mysterious happening. The water in baptism is just plain old water—it's not any more

GOD 5 | 124

holy than what comes out of the tap. At the same time, that water means a whole lot more than your daily shower. The bread and wine in communion don't turn into anything other than bread or wine. They aren't just symbols either. These ordinary things, together with the word of God, create a very extraordinary situation where Christ is really present and we are really changed. We know this because Jesus promised it, and Jesus keeps his word.

That's all we have and it's all we need. Titus 3:4-7 reminds us of this exact point: these sacraments are God's gifts to us. We receive God's mercy and grace through them. They enact God's promises to us, and it is our honor and privilege to be a part of them.

Did You Know?

• Baptism and communion are called *sacraments* because they are gifts of God's grace commanded by Christ with a physical element attached.

 How do you feel about the "mystery" of the water, bread, and wine, together with God's word, bringing Christ's presence to you? Has there been a time when a baptism or communion was particularly meaningful to you? If so, tell about it.

A Rich History

The history of baptism and communion is rich in imagery and symbolism that helps believers understand and incorporate God's promises. The stories behind the practices only make the sacraments more powerful and inspiring.

Baptism in particular takes many forms and has many symbols. Some people like to sprinkle water on the baptized, others pour, still others dip, and some fully immerse. Some churches have large pools to submerge people or bubbling pools to symbolize the flowing waters of life.

The church realized early on that while full immersion was the best symbolic representation of the old self being "drowned," it wasn't always practical. At the end of the day, all you really needed for a baptism was some kind of water used with God's word. Since then, different faith traditions have preferred different methods for baptizing.

Maybe you have noticed that many baptismal fonts are eight-sided. This symbolizes the eight people saved on Noah's ark, which reminds us of the way God's people were saved through the water. It also marks the "eighth day" of creation, the Sunday on which Christ was raised from the dead. When we are baptized into Christ's death, we are also baptized into his resurrection.

Communion, meanwhile, has taken on a shape of its own. Early Christians originally celebrated communion as part of a larger meal that included parts of the Passover meal or a family banquet. To keep the communion celebration separate from a group meal (which could get out of control), they were eventually divided, and later the group meal was dropped entirely. The bread and wine, which were the parts of the meal directly instituted by Christ, remain.

Did You Know?

• *Intinction* is the process of dipping the bread into the wine cup or chalice during communion. When a *common cup* is used, everyone is given wine from the same chalice.

The bread and wine, however, take many different forms. Some churches prefer unleavened bread, since that is most likely what Jesus used at the Last Supper. Some churches prefer to break off pieces from one loaf of bread to symbolize that although we are many, we are one in the body of Christ. Other churches use wafers. But really, any kind of bread can be used. For the wine, most churches agree on using a grape-based drink, meaning wine or grape juice do just fine.

The bread and wine are served different ways in different churches too. You might receive a wafer or piece of bread and a wine glass, a piece of bread to dip into the wine, or a common cup for the wine. No matter how they look, however, the water, wine, and bread are all elements in the sacraments that Jesus began and calls us to continue.

What images, symbols, or forms of the water, bread, and wine are most meaningful to you? Why?

The Body of Christ

One of the greatest joys of taking part in the sacraments is that, through them, you are connected to the entire body of Christ. You join in the great celebration of God's gracious love through simple water, wine, and bread.

Think about it: whether it is in a small house church in China, a lavish cathedral in Italy, an indigenous service in Kenya, or a rural parish in Norway, there are believers just like you joining together in a life-giving meal and a faith-affirming bath. We live in a huge, dynamic, sometimes very impersonal world, but Christians the world over still believe together in the grace, love, and forgiveness promised to us in these sacraments.

After all, that's the point of these sacraments. "For you" does not apply to any one person more than another, and no one can do it any better than anyone else. When Jesus promised he would be with us in these sacraments, he meant that he would be with the entire believing church. These actions aren't just symbolic of a promise, they actually live and act out this unified life in Christ. You belong to a big family that is claimed, washed, fed, and loved dearly. There's no better place to be!

PS Every time you wash your hands, remember that you are a child in God's family, no matter how old you are!

Wrap-up

Centering prayer, silence, gratitude, Sabbath-keeping, and the sacraments—these are all powerful, potent ways to experience God in your life. When you integrate these practices into your faith, you have a very strong foundation on which to build your life. Remember that these things are not prerequisites for a healthy faith life but important tools to keep your faith fresh and fervent. They are tried-and-true ways to feed your faith and a testimony to other people of the life you live and the God you serve. Your experience of God helps you go into the world with the strength and courage to live the life Christ has called you to live!

In My Life

- Commit yourself to keeping Sabbath and receiving communion regularly.
- Volunteer to set things up for communion, bake bread, or assist with serving communion.
- Consider ways for your congregation to welcome those newly baptized. Offer to send greeting cards or create a baptismal banner.
- Check into newsletters, books, and other resources your congregation could provide to new parents.
- Keep a list of those baptized and pray for them.
- Add the prayers from the communion and baptism services to your regular prayer life.
- Tell a family member or friend what your baptism means to you.

129 | GOD 5

Disciple 1

How do I live as a disciple?

Journaling

Key Text: Mark 6:30-32
Key Idea: Journaling as a faith practice provides time to recognize God's everyday blessings and presence in our lives, our role in the world, and God's vision for us.

Step-by-step: Journaling

Preparation: Select a journal or notebook. Find a quiet, comfortable place with minimal intrusions.
Tools and materials needed: your journal and pen or pencil
Time: a few minutes to one hour

1

Take a moment to clear your mind, perhaps shutting your eyes and breathing deeply in and out a few times.

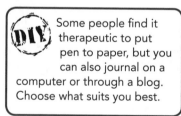

Some people find it therapeutic to put pen to paper, but you can also journal on a computer or through a blog. Choose what suits you best.

2 Write down your thoughts. Don't worry about perfect sentences. If it's difficult to start writing, try one or more of these suggestions:

- List three to five blessings you are thankful for.
- Note one thing you would like to release from your mind—a conflict, troubling moment, embarrassing thing you did or said, or a shortcoming. Name it and let it go. Consider crossing it out boldly.
- Describe what's happening in the world and in your life.
- Describe how your faith is being challenged or nurtured, or your role in God's world and God's vision for you within it.

3 End in prayer.

 How do your journaling thoughts differ from your prayers? During what times in life are you most likely to journal?

Come Away for a While

For six days, God created. "And on the seventh day God finished the work that he had done, and he rested on the seventh day from all the work that he had done. So God blessed the seventh day and hallowed it, because on it God rested from all the work that he had done in creation" (Genesis 2:2-3). Likewise, at the giving of the Ten Commandments, the days of creation and the day of rest were remembered: "Remember the Sabbath day, and keep it holy" (Exodus 20:8). These passages are highlighted in lesson 4, Sabbath keeping, in the God unit.

Journaling as a faith practice is easily implemented as a Sabbath time. Even Jesus knew the need for rest and contemplation. In Mark 6:30-32, as his disciples report back from their evangelistic mission, he gathers them to a deserted place to be alone: "The apostles gathered around Jesus, and told him all that they had done and taught. He said to them, 'Come away to a deserted place all by yourselves and rest a while.' For many were coming and going, and they had no leisure even to eat. And they went away in the boat to a deserted place by themselves."

Christ's care for his disciples included time to cease work, rest, and reflect.

In the midst of hurrying and scurrying, it is easy for us to be caught up in rushing around from one thing to the next—without pausing to reflect, dream, dissect, and hope.

All this coming and going can make it difficult to be thankful for God's blessings, both large and small. Journaling as a faith practice gives us permission to sit quietly, to contemplate for a while. It provides perspective on anxieties and conflicts, allowing us to work through things in a safe place. Journaling allows us time to recognize God's everyday blessings and presence in our lives, simple things that can be easily forgotten in an unexamined life.

Journaling is a pause, an opening to be mindful of our role in God's world and God's vision for us within it. In the midst of this pause, we can see God's hand at work in our lives and in the world.

 How might God work through journaling time to reach you? What could more contemplative rest bring to your life and faith?

Can I Borrow Your Rock?

Before the invention of alphabets, cave dwellers used rocks to scratch the stories of their people in pictographs on rock walls protected from the elements. Surely our genetic ancestors meant to preserve for posterity a record of their struggles and triumphs. Though the format is different, the intention has changed very little.

Through countless generations, individuals have journaled their thoughts and recorded events of the day in varying forms. Some have documented historical journeys. Meriwether Lewis's diary of his expedition across North America with William Clark offers firsthand details of their trek and encounters with native peoples. Presidents and other world leaders often kept journals as a record of their tenure and judgment. Certainly all of these journals have been written with an eye to the future.

Perhaps the journals of the famous seem less intriguing than those of ordinary citizens who wrote for their own benefit, not for history. Through their words we have a window into another era in time. Occasionally ordinary citizens become famous (often posthumously) because of their journals, such as young Anne Frank, a Jewish girl who hid with her family from the Nazis during World War II.

In past centuries, journaling might have consisted of a simple notation on the date in a calendar diary. Over time, journaling evolved as a means of

Did You Know?

• A written journal should be kept in a protected place and include instructions on what to do with it when you are deceased. Consider whether or not you want your descendants to read your thoughts or if you want your journals to be destroyed after your death.

reflection. Now, the Internet has expanded the concept of journaling to include Web logs or blogs, thoughts often targeted for an audience.

Present in all people, but more powerful in some, is the urge to tell one's story, to see one's life recorded for posterity or simply for clarity, to understand one's place in God's universe. Whether done with rock, quill, ink, or Internet, the journal freezes a moment in time and saves it at least for a while.

 Whose journals have you read? What do they teach about the writer's faith? What would inspire you to journal?

Journaling for the Ages

A single mom with two children is journaling their lives and passing on her faith, and she doesn't even know it. She liked the idea of scrapbooking, but couldn't afford all the supplies. Her solution: two desk calendars from the local discount store, one for each child. She glues their drawings, photographs, and other mementos into the date books. But more importantly, each night after she tucks her children in, she sits down with the calendars and writes a little. She hopes to give the children years' worth of calendars when they have children of their own, so she writes to them as adults in the future. In the midst of descriptions of the funny things they say, records of first steps and first grades, are words that tell them just how God has blessed her through them.

Being a single mother is overwhelming at times. Her circumstances (not to mention her checkbook) could hardly be called "blessed." Yet her daily calendar entries identify all the countless little blessings that add up to much joy and thankfulness to God. She notes her prayers for her children. She writes tidbits of scripture—they're meant to help the children keep rooted in their faith as adults, yet she finds they have added to the depth of her own.

The two calendars sitting high on her dresser have become a part of her discipleship. She can't ship off to a foreign country to be a missionary, but she can teach the children in her home and remind them of their roots of faith even after she is gone.

Wrap-up

Journaling as a faith practice allows us to pause to recognize God's everyday blessings and presence in our lives, our role in the world, and God's vision for us. While journaling is generally done on your own, the next faith practice, confession and

 Make journaling a part of your routine. Alert members of your household that, barring emergency, journaling time is sacred and you are not to be disturbed.

forgiveness, can be used on your own, privately with a confessor, or corporately in a worship service.

In My Life

- Use journaling as a way to reflect on the life God has given to you. How is God present and active in your life? Where is God leading you? Write as if you are telling your own story to yourself when possibly you are too old to remember the details.
- Stash your journal in the bathroom vanity, a night-stand drawer, or another location where you'll run across it during the day.
- Buy a journal for any others in your home—including children. Try journaling simultaneously at bedtime or after a meal. Consider sharing with each other one thing that each of you wrote.
- Copy your list of blessings onto a note and attach it to your refrigerator. Invite other household members to do the same.

How do I live as a disciple?

Confession and Repentance

Key Text: Psalm 32:5
Key Idea: In the practice of confession and repentance, we identify our sins to God and God releases us from them.

Step-by-step: Confession and Repentance

Confession and repentance may be done corporately in a worshiping body, one-on-one with another believer, or individually in prayer to God.

Preparation: none
Tools and materials: Bible, pen, and paper (optional)
Time: the duration of a worship service or longer

1 Know your sins. Be honest with yourself and God. Identify your sins mentally, aloud, or on paper.

2 Utilize scripture, prayer, and quiet meditation as part of your confession.

3 Make confession and express repentance.

 Write, "Create in me a clean heart, O God" (from Psalm 51) on a soap dish or pump in your bathroom. Use those fifteen seconds of scrubbing as a time of faithful confession.

4 Celebrate God's grace and forgiveness.

If you are sorry for what you've done wrong, why might confession still be important? Can you be faithful without remembering every single thing you did wrong? How does confession to God differ from confessing a wrong to another person?

A Spirit of Repentance

At three points in the Gospels, Jesus is recorded giving the church the authority to pronounce the forgiveness of sins (Matthew 16:19; Matthew 18:18; John 20:23). This authority is known as the Office of the Keys. This gift to the church shows that absolution, while between the believer and God, is also entrenched in the faith community. Seldom is sin isolated within the heart of a believer; rather, it intermingles with life and all its facets.

As long as you are living, you will never be able to cease sinning. A spirit of repentance names this state and frees you to live in God's grace. Nonetheless, there is a need for true atonement—the real desire to cease the sinful behavior and, subsequently, to make right what has been hurt by your sin.

Confession should not be used as an excuse to continue damaging behaviors or thoughts, even if there is perpetual confession immediately following. Using another Christian as a confessor may keep you honest in this regard.

There is no magic formula to confession and it is not necessary to recall every detail precisely. Confession, intertwined with repentance, shows a desire to live a life of faithful discipleship, even when stumbling along. In Jeremiah, the Lord says, "I am merciful . . . I will not be angry for ever. Only acknowledge your guilt, that you have rebelled against the LORD your God" (Jeremiah 3:12,13). The God we confess to is full of grace and mercy!

Martin Luther and the Reformers understood confession as something that should be done relentlessly throughout the life of the individual. However, they also believed that repentance and confession could be seen in a new light. No longer did confession require a priest as intermediary between an individual and God. Instead, something as simple as the

Did You Know?

• Repentance means being sorry, which means making an honest effort to cease the sin. Confession without true repentance becomes an empty exercise.

Lord's Prayer could serve as a tool of confession. The details in the confession were not as important as the acknowledgement of the presence of sin in a believer's life: "Hear my prayer, O LORD; give ear to my supplications in your faithfulness; answer me in your righteousness. Do not enter into judgment with your servant, for no one living is righteous before you" (Psalm 143:1-2).

What happens when you become caught up in a checklist style of confession? Why might the spirit of repentance be more important than the actual words used? What effect might the presence of a confessor have in a time of private confession?

A Long History

Confession in some form may be just about as old as sin. Jewish and Christian traditions have continually utilized confession as a religious practice. The first book of the bible contains a somewhat forced confession by Adam to God when God's commands are broken. (See Genesis 3, especially verse 12.)

Since sinning didn't end there, neither did the need for confession and repentance. Worship has usually included these elements, beginning at least with the psalms. These 150 songs of praise to God, probably originally used for individual and group worship, frequently contain words of confession and repentance, as well as celebration of God's steadfastness and forgiveness despite humanity's sinful state.

The Protestant Reformation of the sixteenth century focused a great deal on confession as a faith practice to be done frequently in worship, to a confessor, and in prayer to God.

In the long history of repentance and confession as a faith practice, it has occasionally taken an abhorrent turn, such as in the use of flagellation (whipping) and other afflictions as penance for sin. Confession, though sometimes agonizing to the soul, should never be torturous.

A more positive use of repentance and confession emerged in recent years. Countries such as South Africa have utilized confession and repentance as part of the healing process following years of brutality under the rule of apartheid. Archbishop Desmond Tutu of the Anglican Church of Southern Africa headed the South African Truth and Reconciliation Commission. Perpetrators were able to make confession of their crimes with impunity simply for the sake of individual and national healing. Other countries have since followed South Africa's example.

Most often, repentance and confession are lived out as individual and corporate acts of worship, a means of acknowledging human sinfulness and embracing God's grace.

Did You Know?

• *Confession* is a declaration or disclosing of any wrong done. *Repentance* is a feeling of remorse or contrition for a sin.

 How do you see confession and repentance as a faith practice woven into society around you? What difference does it make to know that all believers throughout time have required confession and repentance?

Guilty as Charged

How many times growing up did you hear something like, "Tell your brother (or sister or cousin or friend) you're sorry"? The lessons of our youth should not be lost in adulthood. Offering a heartfelt apology may be a difficult thing to do, but repentance and confession is often the first step toward reconciliation and healing.

Josh knows about confession. He did that in the police interrogation room after the car accident. His delayed reaction to a red light, caused by smoking pot and drinking beer before getting behind the wheel, took the life a young woman and her small daughter. At nineteen, Josh knew his life was changed forever. After sentencing, Josh was sent to the state penitentiary located two hours from his home and his pregnant wife.

Now, years later, Josh lives with his little family determined to make good on the rest of his life. At his sentencing hearing, something happened that changed him and helps him stay clean and sober—he met the man who lost his wife and daughter in the crash. Weeping so hard he could barely speak, the man asked Josh if he could visit him in the penitentiary.

Josh hesitantly agreed. Over the months, the two men grew to know each other. One day, Josh realized he had confessed to God and the court but never really repented. So he did, speaking every conflicted thought right to the face of the man who needed to hear it most. Nothing can bring back the man's wife and daughter, but Josh's repentance made the void just a little more bearable.

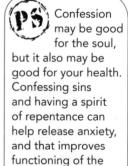 Confession may be good for the soul, but it also may be good for your health. Confessing sins and having a spirit of repentance can help release anxiety, and that improves functioning of the immune system.

Wrap-up

In confession and repentance, we identify our sins to God and strive to not repeat those sins. Our merciful and gracious God grants us forgiveness. In the next practice, we ask for and grant forgiveness to others.

In My Life

- Write your sins on slips of paper, confess them to God, then release them into a fire or shred them into the recycling bin.
- Take a few minutes at home to confess your sins to God. Follow up by making amends. Start by dropping a note or sending an e-mail to say, "I'm sorry."
- Stop and say, "I'm sorry" and explain your wrong when you realize you have sinned against God or another person. Don't wait!

Disciple 3

How do I live as a disciple?

Forgiveness

Key Text: Luke 17:3-5
Key Idea: The practice of
forgiveness is vital to our
relationships with one another.

Step-by-step: Forgiveness

Preparation: none
Tools and materials: communication devices and a Bible (optional)
Time: In some cases, this process takes a few minutes. In others, it takes much more time.

1 Reflect, pray, or seek God's counsel through scripture. If you have wronged someone else, pray for forgiveness. Know who has offended or sinned against you and understand your complicity in the situation, when applicable.

2 Ask for forgiveness from the person you sinned against. Be accountable for the consequences and seek healing by righting wrongs whenever possible. Offer forgiveness to the person who sinned against you.

3 Accept forgiveness with gratitude when offered. Forgive and forever release the person from the burden of the sin.

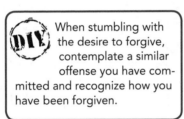

When stumbling with the desire to forgive, contemplate a similar offense you have committed and recognize how you have been forgiven.

Do you find it harder to forgive or be forgiven? Why? What should you tell someone sincerely asking for your forgiveness if you are not truly ready to forgive? Do you think it's a sin to delay forgiveness?

As Many Times as It Takes

Forgiveness is one of the central themes of the Bible, emphasized especially in the New Testament and culminating in the death and resurrection of Jesus Christ. Forgiveness is part of the Christian's practice of being reconciled to one another. We seek love and forgiveness from Christ, and then we turn what we have been given out into the world.

In Matthew 7:12, Jesus says: "In everything do to others as you would have them do to you; for this is the law and the prophets." God freely forgives us because of Christ and his promise, not because of our flawless confession or ability to change our ways. We seek to forgive because we have been forgiven time after time.

Human nature drives us to revenge, but Christ taught us reconciliation. The depth of the forgiveness that Christ calls us to offer extends to all people, even our enemies. It takes a great deal of strength to offer this kind of forgiveness, but the willingness to forgive and be forgiven is an essential faith practice and part of Christ's commandment to love your neighbor as yourself (Matthew 22:39).

In the gospels, Jesus is questioned several times about forgiveness. His answer in Luke 17:3-5 does not dismiss

Did You Know?

• Sometimes an offender denies responsibility or the situation creates an unsafe environment. In these instances, consider forgiving from afar and creating a safe distance between you and the offender.

accountability for offenses, but shows that where there is
repentance, faith demands forgiveness time and time again,
even to a ridiculous extent.

 *How do we forgive repeatedly without becoming a
doormat? What things are the most difficult to forgive?
Why are we more likely to hold grudges against family
and close friends?*

To Begin Again

The history of forgiveness as a faith practice initially seemed
to hinge on God endlessly forgiving humans, as recorded
in the Old Testament or Hebrew Bible. Forgiveness encom-
passed sin and also included issues of property and the
means to earn a living as well. The concept of *Jubilee*,
recorded in Leviticus 25 and following, instructed believers
to forgive debt and return land to original owners every fif-
tieth year. The forgiveness of sins and the forgiveness of debt
served a common purpose of renewal.

The concept of Jubilee has resurfaced through advocacy
for debt cancellation to highly-indebted countries where debt
service inhibits such basic governmental services as health,
education, and food distribution. In this case, Jubilee, like
the individual forgiveness of sins, releases countries from the
chains that bind and allows them to begin again.

For two millennia, Christian churches have celebrated the forgiveness of sins in the sacraments of Holy Baptism and Communion. These marks of the faith community lift up that Christ's death and resurrection was for the forgiveness of sins. No matter how often we sin, through Christ's power in these sacraments we are given a fresh start and begin again.

Proverbs 24:29 states, "Do not say, 'I will do to others as they have done to me; I will pay them back for what they have done.'" Forgiveness, as celebrated by Jews and Christians, is inherently a countercultural act. It has been a powerful force in the world, especially in countries such as Namibia and South Africa, where people have experienced oppression and then forgiven the oppressors when the tables were turned.

Some sins are extremely difficult to forgive: rape, child molestation, abuse, murder, and so forth. Yet examples of victims forgiving their perpetrators abound, such as Pope John Paul's forgiveness to his would-be assassin.

Forgiveness is misused when repeatedly forgiving means offensive behavior continues. Does forgiving mean forgetting? No, it doesn't always make sense to forget a sin, even if you have forgiven the sinner. You can forgive, perhaps from a distance, without putting yourself or another in harm's way.

Did You Know?

• Sometimes we're tempted to bring up a past wrong to make a point in a current conflict. But forgiven wrongs that continue to rear their ugly heads from time to time aren't really forgiven.

What is the greatest example of forgiveness you know, and how does it inspire your faith?

Is Forgiveness Always Possible?

Henry is a man in his mid-thirties. For many years, he held a dark secret inside. From the time he was a small child until his teenage years, his stepfather and mother sexually, physically, and emotionally abused him. As an adult ready to be married and start his own family, he finally spoke the truth to his fiancée. After time in therapy, he talked to his sister for the first time about their shared experience. Eventually, he told his father what had happened and, with time, was able to speak freely about those horrible events and the deep effect they will always have on his life.

Part of the healing process for Henry was gathering in a safe place with his sister and the abusive mother and stepfather. Together, the grown children recounted what had happened and told the perpetrators how horrible it had been and what scars remain. The victims sought accountability—acknowledgement of the sins committed and a pledge to seek professional help if they were to remain a part of the lives of their adult children.

The two parents refused to admit they had done anything wrong or acknowledge the effects of their actions on their children. The meeting ended and years later, the grown children have not spoken to the abusers again.

It is difficult to forgive those who are unrepentant. Henry felt he could not do it himself, so he prayed for God to do it for him. Henry's measure of peace about his past comes from believing that God can forgive even when we cannot.

Wrap-up

The practice of forgiveness—forgiving and being forgiven—is vital to our relationships with one another. We forgive because God forgives us over and over. The next practice, giving, is a response to all that God has done for us.

 In a notebook or in electronic format, review your day through the lens of forgiveness. Make two columns: things to forgive and things to be forgiven for doing. If possible, use the list as a first step to seeking reconciliation.

In My Life

- Model forgiveness. Let your words and actions teach others about forgiveness as a faith practice. Practice forgiveness at work, in the home, on the road, in your circles of family and friends.
- Consider a time in years past when you didn't forgive someone. Seek out that individual to make reconciliation through a note, phone call, or visit.
- Help a young child learn to ask for, receive, and offer forgiveness.
- Pray about a deep hurt that someone has caused you. Ask for God's help in forgiving what you cannot forgive on your own.

Disciple 4

How do I live as a disciple?

Giving

Key Text: Luke 12:29-34
Key Idea: Giving as a faith practice means sharing with others because God has shared so freely with us.

Step-by-step: Giving

Preparation: Gather supplies and information.
Tools and materials: your calendar, information on
your spending, paper, and pen or pencil
Time: unlimited

1 Reflect on your current giving of time, talents, and resources. Read some of Jesus' many teachings on giving.

2 Explore ways to grow in your giving. Find a niche for your time and talents. Consider increasing your financial giving by one or two percent.

3 Increase your giving of time, talents, and resources in ways that reflect your deepening discipleship. Seek out a giving partner and discuss the faith practice, pray for one another, and challenge one another to make giving a regular habit.

DIY Giving starts at home. If you feel you don't have the luxury of donating your time and resources to a great cause, turn off the beeping, flashing electronics and give your time and attention to people you love.

Why is it so difficult to give money and time? Whose spirit of giving inspires you? How would you like to change your spirit of giving?

Where the Heart Is, the Wallet and Calendar Are Sure to Follow

Jesus taught that what you value most in life ultimately becomes your god. Not coincidentally, Jesus had a great deal to say about money. The Gospels record Jesus teaching on the intersection of faith and wealth as much as any other topic.

Stewardship is the care of something that has been entrusted to you. We talk about stewardship of time and talents because they are gifts that God has entrusted to us to use wisely. Giving as a faith practice is ultimately living out the understanding that what has been shared with us so freely, we should also share with others. Giving away ten percent of our financial resources is a commendable goal. But Christ's words remind us that the other ninety percent isn't separate from our faith.

If the bank account of every congregation overflowed and no church ever worried about paying bills, if there were no hungry people in the world, no one in any kind of need, Christians would still be called to give of their resources. It is not God's need to receive that drives our stewardship, but our need to give as a response to our faith in God.

In Mark 12:41-44, Jesus watches as people in the crowd donate money. Wealthy people contribute large sums, while a widow with no visible means of support donates two small coins worth about a penny. The rich people gave what they could afford—their leftovers—but the widow gave all she had. The woman shows us that giving isn't meant to be easy, but giving of our selves and our resources is a heartfelt act of faith.

Jesus' words about money and possessions often sound harsh to our ears. When he instructs followers to sell possessions (Luke 12:33) and give freely to those who are poor, he teaches that the things of this world are fleeting, but God's treasure is forever. We prioritize what flows from our lives as a reflection of our faith in God, so that we may give as freely as we have received.

 What are your biggest challenges in financial stewardship? Are you more inclined to give leftovers or give all you have? Why?

Time, Talent, and Chickens

In ancient times, many cultures practiced a "giving back," to whatever god was worshiped, through sacrifices of crops, animals—and occasionally humans. The Old Testament records the practice of giving sacrifices in thanks and worship to God.

When sacrifices of crops and animals were made, clearly God did not need the food, so often the provisions were distributed to people who were poor and hungry. In Paul's first letter to the Corinthians, this issue was a point of contention, as new converts debated whether sacrificial animals could be eaten. (See 1 Corinthians 10:28 and following.)

The faith practice of giving "first fruits" continues in many agricultural countries today, such as in Christian churches in Africa. The pastor is also frequently "paid" through these gifts to the church—with grains, live chickens, vegetables, and so on. For those believers who have no money or crops to give, a typical practice is to walk to the altar and pause, signifying the giving of oneself.

In past eras, giving was compulsory in many regions of the world. A portion of one's income or harvest went to the ruler or perhaps, living in a feudal system, a tithe went to the landowner. Though this secular practice generally has been replaced by more formal systems of taxation, the metaphor remains: giving as a faith practice, whether of time, talents, or money, signifies giving back to our King.

Giving as a faith practice is sometimes considered optional. Teachings on giving time and resources to God to and through the church are all too often met with disdain. With the world vying for our time and money, it has become increasingly easy to disregard the faith practice of pouring ourselves out for others, but it is no less important.

With many people practicing faithful giving, it makes sense that occasionally you will be on the receiving end. Many individuals find receiving help and gifts from others, especially in times of need, extremely humbling. Yet part of the faith practice of giving is graciously allowing others to help you in turn. You would probably give the shirt off your back to help at least a few people in the world; why not let them reciprocate for you? Giving as a faith practice may occasionally mean putting aside your pride to allow others to help you.

How would giving as a faith practice be different if it were compulsory? Why are so many people better at giving than receiving?

Joy in Giving

They are not wealthy. Their house has been not-quite-finished for twenty years, but they run their own business, raised a couple kids, and found that time has a way of slipping by without all the projects getting done. It would be possible to spend every waking minute of the day involved in the family business, but Liz and Denny are at church more days than not anymore. They serve as mentors for confirmation, keep up the church maintenance, assist during worship, and volunteer on a handful of boards and committees that undergird the work of the church. The couple spends so much time at church that no one would blame them if they didn't toss a cent into the offering plate. But Denny and Liz have found that the more their involvement in their faith community has increased, the more they want to give. Now, even with two kids in college, they tithe their income to the church: ten percent, straight off the top. Liz confesses that at first she thought it might work a little magic, that God would make their business thrive so they wouldn't miss the money. But instead of magic, she found joy in giving. Liz and Denny talk freely about their tithing and they challenge others to try it too. It's not easy, it doesn't mean all financial challenges will evaporate, but it may help life take on an entirely new perspective as you sign that first check of the month.

 Many churches and charitable organizations make it quite easy to set up automated giving so a designated amount comes directly out of your checking account. Utilize this resource to turn giving into a regular habit.

Wrap-up

In the faith practice of giving we share with others the time, talents, and resources God has so freely given us. The next practice, daily humble service, also focuses on others, as we put our neighbors before ourselves for the sake of God's love.

In My Life

- Be mindful of God-given gifts in your life. Show a spirit of thankfulness through your willingness to share these gifts with others.
- Reflect on who has given their time, energy, and resources to you when you needed help the most. Write a thank-you note expressing your gratitude.
- Cross one meaningless event off your calendar this month and use the time instead in service to others in some way.
- Pick up extra food for your local pantry when you shop for groceries, or donate a percentage of your grocery bill to help people in need.
- If you shop at a large discount store, look at the items in your cart before you go through the checkout. Put back any extras and purchase toiletries or diapers for a shelter or pantry instead.
- Tithe your income for one week.

Disciple 5

How do I live as a disciple?

Humble Service

Key Text: Micah 6:6-8

Key Idea: Humble service is the practice of serving others through everyday acts of discipleship.

Step-by-step: Humble Service

Preparation: none
Tools and materials needed: none
Time: often just a few minutes

1 Pray at the start of your day, asking God to touch the lives of strangers and acquaintances through you.

2 Go through your day noting moments and opportunities to be a reflection of God's love—even if just for a moment.

3 Let service—doing justice, loving kindness, walking humbly with God—become an ingrained, faithful habit.

 Use a small notebook or a P.D.A. to track random opportunities for service to others. Is there a pattern to those moments? Consider how you might increase their frequency.

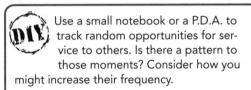 *Where do you think you can easily find opportunities to exercise humble service? What are the biggest challenges to living humbly?*

A Shining Example

Many believers are bogged down with the idea that great faith must come through great acts, forgetting that Christ's example to us was of humble service to the world. Small acts of faithful discipleship in humble service to the world may be the greatest response to God's outpouring of love for us.

In Micah 6, the writer recalls that ceremonial sacrifices are not what God desires from us, but rather a life filled with doing justice, loving kindness, and walking humbly with God. Jesus was the ultimate fulfillment of this humble service. The Savior King was born among the stable animals to a humble girl. He knew no throne and wielded no sword. Jesus surrounded himself not with wealthy and powerful people, but often with those who were outcast and unworthy. He died humbly on the cross and then was laid in another man's tomb. He is our example of humble service that changed the world.

The fifth petition of the Lord's Prayer—"forgive us our sins as we forgive those who sin against us"—is a succinct daily reminder that being humble is a good way of life for sinners who have been granted life and forgiveness by our Creator. As Christ humbled himself for love of us, we are called to serve our brothers and sisters, clothing ourselves with humility in service, for "God opposes the proud, but gives grace to the humble" (1 Peter 5:5).

Like Jesus' parable of the Good Samaritan in Luke 10:25-37, we are called to an everyday, humble, loving service to others that does not put ourselves or our own needs at odds with the needs of others. Often, this faith practice will be contrary to the expectation of a culture that teaches "me first."

You are human; Christ was human and divine. You will never be perfectly humble or live a life of faultless service. The goal is not perfection but discipleship in the midst of everyday living.

Review Micah 6:6-8. What are the ceremonial sacrifices of this era that take our energy away from doing justice, loving kindness, and walking humbly with God? What does Christ's example of humble service mean to you?

Hero Servants, Sung and Unsung

There have always been servants among us, people whose often unsung actions remind us what we are to be about as followers of Christ. Through their lives, we have seen a glimmer of God's love through their everyday discipleship. They have made the world a better place to be simply by looking beyond themselves and outward to the world, both near and far.

In the United States, the many hands and homes of ordinary and faithful church members helped move escaped slaves through the Underground Railroad.

Those who risked their lives for the sake of sheltering and saving Jews during World War II are known as The Righteous Among the Nations. This group includes Italian nuns who hid Jews in their convents; Oskar Schindler, who put refugees to work in a Polish factory; and the entire Dutch village of Nieuwlande, in which every household hid an individual or family. We will never know how many lives were saved because of people like these.

The beauty of faithful disciples such as Mother Teresa of Calcutta is not that they do one grand thing only one grand day, accomplishing an act of service that will stand for a lifetime. Rather, individuals like Mother Teresa spent each day living out small acts of faith through humble service that touched countless lives.

You don't have to be a saint to do goodness in Christ's name. As Martin Luther said, we are freed by the blood on the cross from the power of sin and death—freed to become servants of all.

The world hungers for goodness in the midst of war, genocide, greed, hunger, disease, and distress. Yet with

Did You Know?

• The book and subsequent movie "Pay It Forward" built on the idea of repaying kindness exponentially forward instead of paying back the giver. Imagine using the same model for humble Christian service to the world!

all of this suffering and affliction, so much good is within our reach. How many people do you encounter each day? In each interaction, there is the possibility of humble service, and the cumulative effect of many small things can change the world.

How do you push yourself to look outward to the world instead of only inward? What does it mean to you to be freed to be a servant to all?

Tools of the Trade

Everyone should have a Marie in his or her life. She doesn't look like much sitting at command central—the big table in her kitchen. Within reach are just about all the tools she needs, including phone, note cards, recipes, sewing basket, Bible, and the newspaper. If she sees your name in the local paper, she'll cut out the article and mail it to you with a note reminding you that you're a beloved child of God. When your dog dies, Marie sends a sympathy card and puts your dog's name on her prayer list. When you're down and out, she bakes banana bread and calls you to come pick up your loaf so she can get you in the door for a long talk. For a new baby, there will be a quilt, but only if you bring the baby over for a visit so she can lay her hands on the newborn's head and say a blessing into a future she will never see.

Marie doesn't get out much; she hasn't been able to walk unassisted in years. Nonetheless, many of the children she taught in kindergarten and Sunday school know she's alive and kicking because she continues to reach out to them with humble acts of service. She's not stuffing new hats and mittens in the sleeves of kids whose parents don't have the money any more, but she's still warming hearts on winter days.

Wrap-up

Discipleship takes on many forms, many of which can be interwoven into the roles and interactions that make up our lives. Confession, repentance, and forgiveness undergird our relationships with God and one another and are central to our experience as worshiping communities. Giving and humble service are tools for expressing and living out faith. Journaling can serve as a reflective tool for all of these. We live our discipleship by God's grace, learning and practicing these tools and accepting God's forgiveness when we fail.

 The beauty of daily humble service as a faith practice is that it doesn't wrangle for more of your time or energy. Christian service to others may simply be a way of life.

In My Life

- Consecrate a bracelet or some other symbolic and visible reminder that you are a representative of God's humble service in the world. Wear it daily. Tell others its purpose when asked.
- Make an anonymous donation to a local charity or person in need. Sign an accompanying note, "In God's humble service."
- Express your gratitude for someone performing a volunteer, low-paid, or under-paid service to the community around them, such as child care providers, nursing home staff, community volunteers, and so on.
- Keep a couple lunch sacks of non-perishable food and a beverage in your vehicle for times that you encounter homeless or hungry individuals.
- Give someone a break today; remind him or her of God's love through word or action. Make funny faces at the crying baby on the airplane, let someone go in front of you in traffic or the check-out line, take the worst parking spot.
- Choose an ordinary day on your calendar to be especially mindful of opportunities for humble service in your day. If space allows, write, "Do justice, love kindness, walk humbly with God" on your calendar. The night before this chosen day, write "H.S." (for "humble service") on some sticky notes and place them in strategic places such as in your wallet, on a bathroom mirror, on your front door, on the dash of your car, on your cell phone. Go through your day looking for opportunities for humble service. Let your notes bring you back on track when you get distracted.

How do we celebrate the life and mission of the church?

Prayer for Others

Key Text: James 5:13-16
Key Idea: Through the practice of intercessory prayer, we grow closer to one another and to God.

Step-by-step: Prayer for Others

Prepare: Choose your time and place. It could be solitary and quiet or gathered with a congregation of hundreds or thousands.
Tools and materials: a prayer list (optional)
Time: unlimited

1 Address God: This can be as poetic as "Holy and sovereign God, who breathes life into dry bones..." or as simple as "Lord...."

2 Pray for the church (your own congregation, church leaders, and for the whole church), the world (your local community, as well as national and global concerns), those in need (anyone who is sick or dying or lonely), and for the saints (people who passed on the faith to you and have died).

 Intercessory prayer (praying for someone else) can be as simple and short as you need. Just ask God for whatever is needed and pray for God's will to be done.

 Have people ever prayed for you in a time of need? What effect did this have on your relationship with God or with those who prayed for you?

The Prayer of the Righteous

The Bible is full of references to prayer, including praying for one another (intercessory prayer). Paul's letters feature his promises to pray for the various churches and his appeals that they pray for him. Notice especially Romans 15:30-32 and Ephesians 6:18-20. In Acts 3:1-10, Peter heals a crippled beggar by praying to God on his behalf.

The writer of James offers guidance for people of faith in how they should respond when they are in need. He closes his letter, in fact, with an encouragement to the church to pray for one another. Since they are his closing words, we can assume he thought they were pretty important. Starting in James 5:13, he tells those who are suffering to pray and those who are cheerful to sing songs of praise (which are really prayers of thanksgiving). Then he asks, "Are any among you sick?" and tells us that, if we are sick, we should ask that the elders of the church come to pray over us. Finally, in James 5:16, he reminds all of us to pray for one another and combines it with a promise that the prayer of the righteous is powerful and effective.

Did You Know?

• The healing that God provides and for which we pray is a sign that God's kingdom is being fulfilled. God's healing is evidence of the kingdom. See Luke 10:8-9.

When it seems that prayers are not being answered, we are told to keep praying, and maybe to look for an answer that might surprise us. God promises to answer our prayers, but not always the way we expect.

Prayer, especially prayer for those in need, has been a mark of the church from biblical times, to post-biblical ancient times, to Martin Luther, and to today. A mark of the church means that the activity or practice marks the church as "the church." You know that when you see a group of people praying to God for healing and peace and strength in the name of Jesus, you are seeing the church.

 What does it mean that the prayer of the righteous is powerful and effective? Does it mean that prayers for healing will always be answered with physical healing?

As Ancient as Need

The history of prayer is as long as the history of people. The first recorded prayer is in Genesis 14:19-20, where the priest-king Melchizedek prays for God's blessing to come on Abram. Abram (later Abraham) is portrayed as one who often talks to God, or prays, for himself, for his family, and for those around him. The story of the destruction of Sodom and Gomorrah (Genesis 18-19) features an extended intercessory prayer by Abraham. He prays that God will not destroy Sodom if there are 50, then 45, then 40, then 30, then 20, and finally 10 righteous people are found within the city. And his prayer works: God promises not to destroy the city if 10 righteous people can be found within it.

Throughout the rest of the Bible, prayer is central: prophets pray for the nation, people pray for their children. The early church recognized intercessory prayer as a key spiritual gift, and it was a primary role of the apostles as leaders of the church (Acts 6:3-4). After biblical times, people in the church and leaders in the church continued to pray.

In fact, the monastic movement was originally motivated, in part, by the desire to pray for the church and the world. The early monks were people who withdrew from society to caves and isolated places in the wilderness (especially deserts) in order to be less distracted by the world. They did this to study and to pray. They felt it was their role to spend their lives in prayer for the church and for the whole world.

Did You Know?

• Some monasteries and churches have practiced "perpetual prayer," having someone in a chapel or prayer room praying 24 hours a day, 7 days a week. Sometimes this is done for a short time, such as Holy Week, and sometimes for dozens of years at a time.

 How would you know if this faith practice of intercessory prayer is one for which you are called and gifted?

Prayer Healers

Many congregations feature prayer ministries. This may involve special worship services with prayers for healing, prayer ministers, a prayer chapel, a prayer chain, or other ideas. At a service for healing, designated prayer ministers are often available to pray one-on-one with worshipers for whatever healing is needed by them or someone they care about. These prayer ministers (who may be ordained pastors but often are not) are available to listen to concerns and to pray for God's healing and strength. Sometimes oil is used to anoint the hands or the head of the one in need of prayer. In the oil, a prayer minister might retrace the cross that was marked in baptism. As the scent of the oil rises, we know our prayers rise to God and the feel of the oil on our skin is a reminder that each of us have been anointed and called God's daughters and sons. While tracing the cross or anointing the hands, the prayer minister may pray something like this: "May the God who called you Beloved provide healing, strength, and wholeness in your time of need. Amen."

Wrap-up

Prayer is a way that the church is marked as the body of Christ, and it is an opportunity to grow closer to God and to one another. Intercessory prayer is a key part of each worship service, as we pray for the church, for the world, for those in need, and in thanksgiving for God's saints who have gone before us.

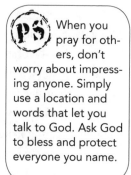

PS When you pray for others, don't worry about impressing anyone. Simply use a location and words that let you talk to God. Ask God to bless and protect everyone you name.

The next practice, worship, is another way that the church is marked as the body of Christ.

In My Life

- Use your congregation's list of prayer concerns to guide your prayer. Many congregations publish such a list. If yours does not, maybe you can help get one started.
- Place a list of people to pray for in your journal or Bible. Pray for these people regularly, and let them know you are praying for them!
- Pray your congregation's directory. Name the names and pray that God will bless and strengthen the people in whatever ways they need. If the directory is very large, just pick one letter: pray for all the Ns, for example.
- When you see an ambulance or hear a siren this week, say a quick prayer for whoever is involved.
- Pray the newspaper. As you read, pause to pray after each story for those involved.

How do we celebrate the life and mission of the church?

Worship

Key Text: Psalm 122:1

Key Idea: The practice of regular worship reminds us who we are as God's children and the body of Christ, strengthens us for the journey, and propels us into action in the world.

Step-by-step: Worship

Preparation: none
Tools and materials: a worship bulletin, hymnal,
or whatever other worship resource will be used
Time: duration of worship service

1 Prepare to participate in all aspects of the worship service.

2 Gather in the name of God by singing, reading a responsive call to worship, remembering your baptism, and/or by confessing sins and hearing words of forgiveness.

3 Hear God's word in the scripture readings and the sermon. (For more on this, see lesson 8 in the Bible unit.)

4 Share the meal. Participate in the offering, prayer, and singing, then receive the Lord's Supper. (For more on this, see lesson 5 in the God unit.)

5 Go out to live a life of faith in the world.

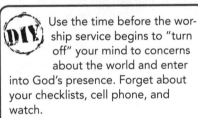

DIY Use the time before the worship service begins to "turn off" your mind to concerns about the world and enter into God's presence. Forget about your checklists, cell phone, and watch.

? *What physical environment do you find most helpful to worship? What is it about that environment that helps you worship? In worship, how do you know you are worshiping God and not just gathering with friends?*

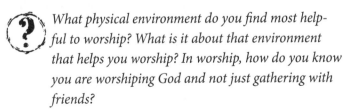

The House of the Lord

When the ancient Hebrews entered into the promised land, they were housing the ark of the covenant in a tabernacle or tent. The ark had things that reminded them of God's presence: the tablets of the law that Moses received at Mt. Sinai and some of the manna that fed them through 40 years in the wilderness. Finally, Solomon built a temple in Jerusalem to house the ark, remind people of God's presence, and be a place where the people could encounter God. That temple was destroyed. The one built to replace it was destroyed by the Romans in the year 70, less than 40 years after Jesus' death.

The ancient Israelites came to the temple to make their yearly sacrifices. Priests and Levites at work in the temple prayed on behalf of the people all year round. Worshiping in the temple was a great joy for the people, just as worshiping in church can be for us. That is why we echo the words of Psalm 122: "I was glad when they said to me, 'Let us go to the house of the LORD!'"

But God's presence is not confined to one place. Jesus said, "Where two or three are gathered in my name, I am there among them" (Matthew 18:20).

Did You Know?

• In the temple and the tabernacle, people gathered in a courtyard to give their offerings and sacrifices. Only the priests carried the sacrifices into the holy place. Only the one high priest could enter the holiest place, where the ark was. And he only did that once a year!

When we gather together with others in the name of God, God promises to be with us.

Tell about the worship experience in which you were most aware of God's presence. Where were you? Were there others with you?

Worship Ancient and New

Early Christians worshiped in houses or catacombs, which were underground cemeteries. It was only in the fourth century, when Christianity was legalized and made the official religion of the Roman Empire, that Christians began to construct church buildings. Because most of the first Christians came from a Jewish background (as did Jesus), much of the structure and words of worship echoed the worship services people had known from the temple and the synagogues. We use many of these same words and forms today.

The benediction "The Lord bless you and keep you, the Lord make his face shine on you…" is the blessing that

Did You Know?

• One of Martin Luther's main reforms to church life was in worship: he wanted people to worship in German (their native language) instead of Latin, which they did not know. He did this so the people could participate in the liturgy.

The word *liturgy* that we use for the words and songs of worship means "the work of the people." Worship and liturgy are your work! Your participation is key.

God commanded Aaron to use in Numbers 6:22-26. The words "Holy, holy, holy, God of power and might…," that we often sing during the Communion liturgy, echo the words of the seraphs in Isaiah 6:3. The Eucharistic Prayers used by the pastor before Communion echo many of the table prayers that Jesus and his followers would have used.

 Does using the same familiar words in worship help you to focus? Why or why not? Why do you think we say or sing quotations from the Bible so often during worship?

Shared Heritage

A group of confirmation students from a Lutheran congregation visited congregations of other faith backgrounds as part of their learning. They visited a Roman Catholic parish for worship as well as other Protestant congregations. The students were all struck by how similar the worship experiences were to those they knew from their own congregation. Many of the same songs were sung, many of the same prayers were prayed, and the overall order of the services was very similar.

One week the students went to a local Jewish synagogue to visit worship. There was much that was different—no references to Jesus, no Communion meal, and scripture was read in a different language, Hebrew. But the students recognized some similarities. They recognized the words of the blessing at the end of the service, and they recognized the psalm that was chanted. Through this worship experience and the conversations that followed, the students learned that worship in their congregation and church denomination is one part of a heritage of worship experiences that stretches back thousands of years.

 What experiences do you have with Christian worship outside your congregation? What are the differences and similarities? What can Christians learn from Jewish worship?

Wrap-up

Regularly gathering to worship with other Christians is central to the life of a disciple. In each gathering, we hear the Word, share the Meal, and get sent to serve. We receive encouragement from knowing we are not walking this path alone.

The next practice focuses specifically on the encouragement we give and receive through the church.

PS We all need regular reminders and regular encouragement from God's word and our fellow believers. Commit to making regular worship in your congregation a part of your life as a disciple.

In My Life

- Commit yourself to attending worship each week for the next month, if this isn't your normal practice. Recommit when the month is up.
- Attend Friday evening worship at a local Jewish synagogue. If you know someone who can go with you to guide the experience, take advantage of that opportunity.
- Volunteer to greet or usher at worship services or to help assemble worship bulletins.
- Write the words "Go in peace to serve the Lord" on a small card and tape it to your bathroom mirror. (These words are often used to bless and send the congregation at the close of worship.) Think about how worship is connected to serving God.
- Use a worship bulletin to identify the four-piece structure of a worship service in your congregation. How do you gather, hear the word, share the meal, and go out into the world?
- Invite someone to come to worship with you.

How do we celebrate the life and mission of the church?

Encouragement

Key Text: 1 Peter 5:12
Key Idea: The practice of encouragement puts God's love into action in the world.

CHURCH 3

Step-by-step: Encouragement

Preparation: none
Tools and materials: none
Time: often just a few minutes

1 Listen to the people around you. What kinds of fears and anxieties are being expressed?

2 Share your own struggles and how God has helped you to overcome them. Note: do this briefly. The focus is on helping and encouraging your neighbor, not in talking about yourself.

3 Offer to help. Ask what you can do. Promise to pray for the person.

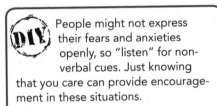

People might not express their fears and anxieties openly, so "listen" for non-verbal cues. Just knowing that you care can provide encouragement in these situations.

When you have felt tired or worn out in your faith journey, what is the most encouraging thing someone has done for you?

Letters of Encouragement

Paul's letters are among the best examples of encouragement in the Bible. Paul never stayed very long in one place. He traveled throughout the known world preaching the gospel of Jesus Christ and starting churches in city after city. Before long, he invariably heard about some snag or problem or disagreement believers were having in one of the churches he had started. He wrote letters to these young congregations—letters of teaching and encouragement—and urged them to remain faithful to what he had taught them and what God had shown them. We have several of these letters in our New Testament today.

Paul tailored his encouraging words to the particular need of each congregation. For example, he encouraged the Corinthians to be united as followers of the one Christ (1 Corinthians 1:10-17). He prayed that the Ephesians would be strengthened in their faith (Ephesians 3:14-19) and that the Philippians would not be worried about him while he was in prison (Philippians 1:12-14).

Paul was, of course, not the only biblical writer or person to offer encouragement. For example, 1 Peter was written to a group of Christians who had undergone great persecution for their faith, simply to encourage

Did You Know?

• Encouragement and consolation share Latin root-words, so when we console those who are grieving or lonely or hurting, we are encouraging their faith.

them to stand firm in faith and believe in God's righteousness (1 Peter 5:12).

 Have you ever gotten a letter, a note, a card, or an e-mail of encouragement? How did it feel to know that someone took the time to write to you?

Stick to the Path

One role of the church (the gathered people of God) has always been to encourage one another to live faithfully in our baptismal promises on the journey of discipleship. From ancient times, preaching has been seen as a way to encourage a congregation and individual members in faith and help them make faithful decisions in life.

Although it took on a very different tone over time, even excommunication (removal of church membership) was first intended as encouragement. Excommunication originally placed people who needed attention and help in a category (and sometimes even physical location), where they could receive special instruction, prayers, and encouragement to return to the church and to the faith.

Over the years, the church developed many ways of encouraging one

Did You Know?

• The sending portion of worship encourages us to go out into the rest of the week blessed by God to serve the Lord.

another and being encouraged in faith and discipleship through ministries of prayer, faith formation, fellowship, justice and action, outreach to those in need, and more.

 Think about a time when you tried to encourage someone's faith. What happened? How did this affect your own faith?

Encouragement Returned

The seniors in the congregation decided they wanted to encourage the young people and let them know they were cared about at church. In the beginning, a few elderly members took it upon themselves to send birthday cards to high school students from the congregation. Soon someone decided that it would be appropriate to send "baptismal birthday" cards on the anniversary of each young person's baptism, encouraging them to stay faithful to the baptismal promises. And it grew from there. Whenever high school students were mentioned in the newspaper for making the honor roll at school or playing in a football game or the marching band, they received cards from the congregation that said something like, "Keep it up. God loves you."

Some time later, the high school students decided to return the encouragement. The youth group got together to send cards from the congregation to seniors on their birthdays and their baptismal birthdays. Students began to visit nursing homes and the hospital. Soon the encouragement was truly intergenerational.

PS Practicing encouragement isn't always easy, but stick with it. A few encouraging words, a "thumbs up" sign, a note, or an e-mail message can make a difference in someone's life.

Wrap-up

No one can walk the journey of faith alone. We need to inspire, encourage, and lift one another up every once in a while. When we practice encouragement, we put God's love into action in the world.

In My Life

- Make a commitment to yourself to be aware of cues in your regular daily life that someone needs encouragement.
- Send a note of encouragement and comfort to someone in your congregation who is in need.
- Get together with others and thank the teachers in your congregation with a special meal or celebration.
- Write or call someone whose encouragement has had a big impact on your life.
- Reach out to a neighbor, friend, or coworker who seems to need someone to talk to. Listen to this person's concerns and offer your prayers.
- Write a note of encouragement to each confirmation student in your congregation.
- Encourage a friend or family member to encourage others.

How do we celebrate the life and mission of the church?

Celebration

Key Text: 2 Samuel 6:12-22
Key Idea: In celebration we give praise for the blessings of God and the joys of the journey of discipleship.

Step-by-step: Celebration

Preparation: varies
Tools and materials: optional, very simple to elaborate
Time: varies

1 Listen to the people around you. What is God doing in their lives? What is God doing in the congregation? Listen for cues to blessings and causes for celebration.

2 Celebrate. Shine light on others and on what God is doing in their lives or in the congregation.

3 Pray and give thanks for God's blessings.

DIY Celebrating the blessings of God is all about attitude and perspective. Next time you are about to say, "I am so lucky…," instead start by saying, "God has blessed me…." It makes a difference.

 What are you most thankful for? Have you prayed a prayer of thanksgiving for this? Have others shared your celebration? What difference would that make?

Dancing like Crazy

After King David secured and built up the city of Jerusalem, he wanted to bring the ark of God from its temporary location to a more permanent place in the city. The ark held reminders of what God did through the exodus from Egypt and the covenant with the people. 2 Samuel 6:12-22 describes the entry of the ark into Jerusalem and the celebration that accompanied it.

David, king of the whole nation, is portrayed like a giddy little child, dancing "with all his might" before the ark as it made its way through towns and villages up into Jerusalem. David danced and shouted and rejoiced as he led the procession. Behind him were people playing trumpets and lyres and tambourines, and all the leaders of the nation singing praise to God for the blessings of the land and of the covenant.

Michal, David's wife, watched the whole event, appalled at the undignified and "un-royal" way her husband was acting. Later that evening she chided him for his behavior, saying that he should have been more dignified and that he had embarrassed himself before all the people and his servants.

Did You Know?

• Many other places in the Bible talk about celebrating God. Here are two examples.

• Even nature celebrates: "The mountains and hills before you shall burst into song, and all the trees of the field shall clap their hands" (Isaiah 55:12).

• We are called to praise God with every instrument we can get our hands on! See Psalm 150.

David's reply is a good reminder when we might feel embarrassed about celebrating and giving thanks. Those who refuse to see what wonderful things God has done are the ones who should be embarrassed.

 Have you ever sung a hymn or song during worship at the top of your lungs, not caring what others might think? What would happen if you did? What would it take for you to dance, sing and shout in response to God's blessings?

Sharing Joys

Throughout Christian history, believers have shared their joys with one another in times of blessing and have celebrated together. We see this in letters that reported on their joys and in days set aside specifically to give thanks for God's blessings.

Some of the best-loved pieces of music, from symphonies to hymns to guitar-based songs, are expressions of celebration. Sometimes these were written to express general celebration of God's goodness, but often they were written to celebrate a particular event.

Wolfgang Amadeus Mozart wrote a "Coronation" mass as a celebration of the coronation of Emperor Leopold II of Austria in 1791. The hymn "How Great

Did You Know?

• On Thanksgiving many churches gather special offerings of food for the hungry. This practice of celebrating God's blessings by sharing with others is as ancient as the worship of God.

 CHURCH 4

Thou Art" was written to celebrate all of God's great creation by Swedish pastor Carl Gustaf Boberg, after his evening walk. The hymn "Amazing Grace" was written by a former slave-trader-turned-Christian minister to celebrate the conversion that God can bring to lives. Each of these pieces of music continues to be used today by people celebrating God's blessings in their own lives.

 Name a favorite hymn or religious song that celebrates God. What is it about that particular music that helps you celebrate?

Celebrating Milestones

A congregation may become involved in observing a member's baptism, wedding, and even funeral (celebrating a life lived in God), but more opportunities are available for honoring key times in people's lives. Many congregations hold additional "milestone celebrations" as reminders that God is the source of all blessing.

Some churches celebrate the milestone of graduation from high school or college with special recognition during a worship service, a gift from the congregation, and prayers of thanksgiving for God's blessings. Other milestones and events in life provide opportunities to share in celebration as well: first communion, confirmation, a new driver's license, the purchase of a first home, retirement, and so on.

Wrap-up

In celebration we share joys with one another in the congregation, knowing that all blessings come from God.

In the next practice, hospitality, we welcome others into the faith community and the journey of discipleship.

PS God has blessed us richly, and when we share those joys and blessings with others, they are multiplied. That's cause for celebration!

In My Life

- Scour your local newspaper for fellow church members mentioned, especially youth in the sports pages or honor roll. Send a card of celebration.
- Organize a "senior prom" event for the senior members of your congregation to celebrate life and relationships. Play big band music and serve dinner or refreshments.
- Bring a gift basket or "care package" from your congregation to a family on the birth or adoption of a child.
- Spend a few minutes sharing joys and saying prayers of thanksgiving at the start of every church committee meeting.
- Begin or carry on a tradition of serving a breakfast to new members and their sponsors.
- Throw a surprise party for the anniversary of your pastor's ordination.
- Celebrate milestones in the congregation's life: a pastor's new call or retirement, start of a new pastor's ministry, ground-breaking for a new building or addition, a special anniversary year, send-off or homecoming for a mission trip, and so on.

How do we celebrate the life and mission of the church?

Hospitality

Key Text: Hebrews 13:2
Key Idea: In hospitality, we respond to God's welcome of us as sinners by welcoming others to share faith and fellowship with us.

Step-by-step: Hospitality

Preparation: Before practicing hospitality, spend some time reflecting on the nature of the church and Christian fellowship. Once you have a handle on this, you can more effectively welcome someone else.
Tools and materials: none
Time: a few minutes or more

1 Listen and watch for people who need to be welcomed. Watch for visitors to your congregation.

2 Smile genuinely and find out whether the person has any questions or needs assistance in any way.

3 Bring the other in. Like all groups, the church has inside groups and its own terminology. Make every effort to expand the circle and welcome new people.

 Practice being aware of group dynamics. Watch for people left out of the circle. Engage them in conversation. Get to know them.

 What is it that brought you to the congregation you are in right now? What was it like the first time you visited? Have you ever felt under-welcomed or over-welcomed? What made you feel that way?

Welcome Angels

Hospitality is one of the most prized human practices in the Bible. Because the countryside was dangerous and there were no hotels in biblical times, it was considered a social and religious obligation to provide shelter and a meal for anyone who came to your home. In the Old Testament, Abraham and Sarah welcomed three strangers into their home (Genesis 18) and the strangers turned out to be angels. The prophets would later remind the people over and over to take care of strangers and aliens who lived in the land.

In the New Testament, the parable of the good Samaritan (Luke 10:25-37) is about hospitality. The Samaritan showed hospitality to the injured man by providing for his needs. Jesus talked about hospitality when he described the final judgment in the parable of the sheep and the goats (Matthew 25:31-46). In these verses Jesus said that we welcome him whenever we welcome a stranger. Finally, the letter to the Hebrews includes advice about hospitality in a list of last-minute reminders about Christian service: "Do not neglect to show hospitality to strangers, for by doing that some have entertained angels without knowing it" (Hebrews 13:2).

Did You Know?

• The word "angel" means messenger from God—any messenger from God. Because strangers remind us of our obligation (from God), all strangers really are angels.

Tell about a time when you heard or saw a reminder of God from a surprising source, such as from a visitor to your church or a person you didn't know. How would it change things if we saw those we don't know and those who are hungry, thirsty, and imprisoned as Jesus?

The Church as Welcoming Sanctuary

In medieval Europe, churches were places of special legal status called "sanctuary." The church was considered a safe space that anyone could enter. If a fugitive from the law entered a church, he or she was given "sanctuary," or safe housing, for a period of 40 days. This sanctuary could not be violated by anyone, not even the king. The 40 day period may have allowed for cooler heads to prevail against a pursuing mob or posse. Sometimes it gave fugitives opportunities to prove their innocence.

Some elements of this heritage continue today, as the contents of a ritual confession between a person and a pastor cannot be shared with the authorities, except in a few cases. In some places a right to sanctuary, similar to medieval practices, is still respected or asserted.

Did You Know?

• Sanctuary was not a "Get out of jail free" card. In medieval times, people would keep watch around the clock for 40 days to ensure a fugitive claiming sanctuary did not escape.

CHURCH 5

In our church buildings, we call the room in which we worship the "sanctuary." Here is a place and a group of people in which we can be safe, where we can be welcomed regardless of our status in life.

 In what ways is your church a sanctuary? Have you ever talked about something at church that you could never talk about anywhere else? What would make you feel welcome and comfortable to do that?

Greeters and Good-Byers

Most congregations have a ministry of hospitality involving greeters, people who stand near the door and welcome everyone, especially those visiting. But some congregations are extending the ministry of hospitality to include "Good-Byers." It is the job of Good-Byers to stand near the doors at the end of the service and welcome visitors again, thanking them for coming and engaging them in conversation. Good-Byers may try to steer visitors to a time of fellowship, introduce them to others, or invite them to an adult study hour.

The worship service often prompts questions and piques interest in visitors. Good-Byers can answer some of those questions and make sure visitors don't just slip out the door. At the very least, newcomers are thanked for their presence at worship and invited to come back again.

Wrap-up

The practice of hospitality helps to make the circle of faith and fellowship larger and share the journey of discipleship with others.

In the next practice, service, we share our blessings and gifts with others.

 We are welcomed into God's family through baptism and continually welcomed into relationship with God and the church. Through the practice of hospitality, we share this welcome with others.

In My Life

- Serve as a greeter at a worship service, even unofficially. Say hello to at least two people you don't know well.
- Put yourself in a visitor's shoes the next time you come to church. Can you find a parking place? Is it easy to find your way into the building and to the sanctuary, fellowship area, and restrooms? Discuss this with the pastor or a church council member.
- Welcome children to worship with cloth bags filled with quiet toys, coloring pages, and crayons.
- Look for ways to make the exterior of your church building more inviting with regular maintenance, banners, seasonal plants, and so on.
- Spend 10 minutes in conversation with someone who has joined your congregation in the last year. Find out what made them feel welcome and why they chose to join.
- Plan a special event at your church and invite the surrounding neighborhood or community to come.

How do we celebrate the life and mission of the church?

Service in and through the Congregation

Key Text: Deuteronomy 26:12-13

Key Idea: Service in and through the congregation allows us to serve God by serving others and sharing our blessings.

Step-by-step: Service in and through the Congregation

Preparation: none
Tools and materials: paper, pen or pencil
Time: unlimited

1 Thank God for your blessings and pray for a way to be a blessing to others.

2 Discover your place(s) for service. List the things you love to do (your passions) and the things you are best at (your talents). Highlight the top two areas where your passions and talents intersect and look for ways to use these.

3 Serve God and be a blessing to others.

 DIY Don't wait to be asked to serve—you are blessed to be a blessing! Look through a worship bulletin or church newsletter or talk to your pastor or another leader about using your top passions and talents to serve in and through your congregation.

What is the committee or area of ministry you are most interested in at the moment? Do you love it? Are you good at it? If you aren't already part of that ministry, what is keeping you from being involved?

First Fruits

Deuteronomy 26:12-13 is one part of the law that God gave to the people of Israel to guide their life in the promised land. God had promised to bring the people to a fruitful land where their lives could be blessed. God expected the people to respond by bringing some of the first fruit (the best, prime produce) from the land to the priest as their offering. That offering would support the Levites (temple workers who had no land of their own), aliens in the land, and those who had been orphaned or widowed.

God seems to have special concern for those who cannot provide for themselves. For example, in Psalm 68:5, God is called "father of orphans and protector of widows." Leviticus 19:9-10 goes on to say that harvesters must leave enough food in the field so that aliens (who have no land of their own) and those who are poor can come and get what they need.

Did You Know?

• Congregations working together is as old as the church itself. Paul took a collection (to benefit the poorer church in Jerusalem) from each of the churches he had started. (See 1 Corinthians 16:1-2.)

 What does God's concern for those who can't provide for themselves say about service? In service in and through the congregation, what would happen if everyone gave the first fruits of their time, talents, and financial resources?

Priesthood of all Believers

Martin Luther reminded the church that all gifts and talents come from God and are intended to be honored and respected as blessings for the sake of the community. Some people are blessed with the talent and passion to clean bathrooms or mow lawns. Those are blessings to the community with just as much dignity as the greatest financial gifts or most beautiful singing voice.

Luther used the term *vocation* or calling to describe these gifts. Some are called to be pastors, some are called to be teachers and writers, some musicians, some custodians, some nursery attendants. The point is that we are all called by the same God, gifted by the same God, and called to use our gifts as blessings to the whole community and the world.

Did You Know?

• Paul recognized early on that each of us has different gifts (1 Corinthians 12:1-11), all given by the same God. Everyone doesn't have to do everything, but by working together and being guided by the Holy Spirit, we can accomplish anything.

What is the job or task in your congregation that nobody wants to do? Why are certain tasks or roles avoided? What is your vocation or calling from God?

Gifts Can Be Surprises

Susan's congregation, like many, provided new members with the opportunity to fill out a spiritual gifts inventory. After answering a series of questions about what she loved to do and her various experiences, Susan was invited to talk with the pastor. Based on Susan's responses to the questions and the conversation, the pastor invited Susan to teach a confirmation class. At first, Susan said no. She was terrified of kids and felt that she didn't have the biblical background to be able to teach them. But finally she agreed to do it on a trial basis.

Twenty years later, Susan has loved every minute of it. And so have the students. They have learned from her, caught her faith and passion, and most importantly, known that someone cares. Susan never would have thought of herself as a confirmation teacher, but it turned out to be the perfect calling for her.

 We were made to serve God and one another. We have been blessed to be a blessing. Service should not be a burden. If it is, find a new area of service.

Wrap-up

Through service in the church, the community of faith, we serve God by serving others.

In the next faith practice, testimony, the church shares the good news of Jesus Christ with others.

In My Life

- Try something new. Respond to the next appeal for volunteers in your congregation. See whether that area of ministry fits you.
- Serve by giving a ten percent tithe of your income to your congregation this week.
- Take a spiritual gifts inventory and identify areas where you will serve.
- Start or join a church group or ministry that allows you to serve with your top passions and talents. Whether you're good at visiting people who are sick or hospitalized, cooking or providing hospitality, getting the word out about your congregation and upcoming events, knitting caps and shawls, taking care of toddlers, or something else altogether, there is a place to serve.
- Mentor a child or youth into the regular practice of service.

How do we celebrate the life and mission of the church?

Testimony

Key Text: Matthew 10:7
Key Idea: In the practice of testimony, we witness to God's love in Jesus Christ.

CHURCH 7

Step-by-step: Testimony

Preparation: none
Tools and materials: paper or journal and writing utensil
Time: varies

You can practice testimony on your own in a variety of settings, but here in the last lesson of the Church unit, the focus is on testimony in and through the congregation.

1

Know your faith story. Consider writing down key points in your journey of discipleship.

2 Tell your story. Participate in an opportunity to witness to God's love in and through your congregation. Let others see God's love shining through you and your church.

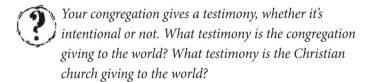

If you can't participate directly in an opportunity to witness to God's love in and through your congregation, consider providing support through your prayers, encouragement, and financial gifts.

Your congregation gives a testimony, whether it's intentional or not. What testimony is the congregation giving to the world? What testimony is the Christian church giving to the world?

As You Go

Jesus sent his disciples out on a mission and gave them very specific instructions. One part of his instructions, in Matthew 10:7, says, "*As you go*, proclaim the good news, 'The kingdom of heaven has come near.'" First of all, we have good news to share. The good news is that God is in charge and God has a plan.

What is often missed is that Jesus says "as you go." Jesus did not tell his disciples, and he surely doesn't tell us, that we have to all go to remote villages as missionaries. He doesn't tell us that we all have to go to seminary and become pastors. He says, "as you go, proclaim the good news." As we go through life, Jesus calls us to proclaim the good news.

Did You Know?

• Testimony is about saying *why* we believe and have hope. 1 Peter 3:15 says you should always be ready to give "an account of the hope that is in you."

 What testimony is given by the normal daily and weekly activities of your congregation?

Whole Body Preaching

What words should the church use to account for the hope that is in us? What are the right words? How can we say this more eloquently, so others will really listen?

Actually, evangelism and testimony are not about the "right words." They're not even all about words. St. Francis of Assisi (1181–1226) said "Preach the gospel at all times—if necessary, use words." What does that mean? The tools of testimony aren't limited to words. Our whole lives, and the life of the congregation, offer testimony. They bear witness to our beliefs and core principles—or at least they should. St. Francis challenges us to make everything we do and say, as individuals and as a congregation, account for our hope and bear witness to the love and grace of God in the world.

Did You Know?

• Francis of Assisi lived what he spoke. The child of a wealthy merchant, Francis left behind a promising career to take a vow of poverty and service.

 How do others in your community know that your congregation is Christian? How can your congregation preach the gospel at all times?

Traveling Testimony

Megan was excited when she heard her youth group was going on a service trip to build homes for people who needed housing. From past experience, Megan knew the youth group would worship in interesting and different ways on the trip, do Bible study together, and talk about God and faith. She liked the idea, but wished that her best friend Kristen could go on the trip too.

Kristen wasn't a member of the congregation, or any church for that matter. When Megan talked to the youth pastor about this, he said Kristen would be welcome to come on the trip.

 How is building homes a testimony to God's love in Jesus Christ? How is inviting someone on a service trip a testimony? Is it easier for you to share your faith with someone you know, or someone you don't know?

Wrap-up

In this unit we have explored faith practices that involve us in the life of the congregation, the community of believers. Through these practices, we celebrate the life and mission of the church and invite others to experience God's love and grace and become part of a faith community.

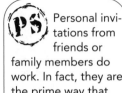

PS Personal invitations from friends or family members do work. In fact, they are the prime way that people become connected to the church.

In My Life

- Think of one person you know who does not have a church home. Invite that person to attend worship or another congregational event with you.
- Look for opportunities to tell a friend, family member, or co-worker what you appreciate most about your congregation.
- Write your faith autobiography and publish it in your congregation's newsletter.
- Think of the person most instrumental in your faith life and write a thank-you letter for his or her testimony.
- Pray regularly for your congregation, its leaders, and the larger church.

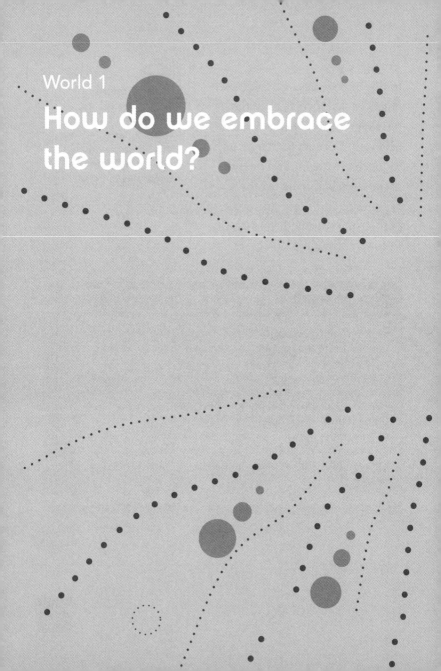

World 1

How do we embrace
the world?

Simplicity

Key Text: Luke 12:22-34
Key Idea: Simplicity is practiced through careful consideration of our belongings, resources, and time.

WORLD 1

Step-by-step: Simplicity

Preparation: none
Materials needed: none
Time: 5-50 minutes

1 Consider your belongings, resources, and time. What significance do they have to you? Could they be used differently?

2 Be conscious when shopping for new items. Impulse purchases may lead you to buy more than you need, especially if you are attracted by a discount price.

 DIY Keep simplicity in mind when you shop for *anything*. Ask yourself: Do I need this? Do I need this quantity? Do I need it in every color available? Is there something I already own that I could use instead?

 Think of one item at home you could donate, throw away, or give to a friend right now. Why are you reluctant to let it go? What do your possessions mean to you?

Fasting and Simplicity in the Scriptures

Fasting or refraining from eating is a spiritual discipline taught through religious history (not only in the Christian church). A fast generally would last a day or longer. Fasting is one way to live a simpler life, by stripping away grand gastronomic excesses, in order to pursue spiritual disciplines. In the Bible, fasting is assumed as a valid spiritual discipline, though not commanded by Jesus. Jesus fasted for forty days and nights before embarking on his messianic mission (Matthew 4:1-2; Luke 4:1-2).

Some people today reject fasting for medical or health reasons, but with the right preparation, most people can participate in some kind of fast. Some use the word "fast" when "giving up something for Lent" ("fasting from chocolate" or "fasting from television," for example). Other people fast from lunch during a certain period of time (a week or once a week) as a way of being in solidarity with the poor and hungry. Eating a simple soup and light bread for dinner can be a way of honoring the simplicity of a fast, without completely abstaining from food.

The New Testament gives other examples of simplicity. Jesus tells the story of the rich fool who hoarded for years and years in order to care for himself. He built bigger barns to house his many harvested crops, but one night, he died. Jesus points out that we can't guarantee our livelihood by hoarding and storing. He encourages his hearers to simplify when he says, "Do not worry about your life, what you will eat or what you will drink, or about your body, what you will wear" (Matthew 6:25). Instead, "strive first for the kingdom of God" (Matthew 6:33).

Through the discipline of simplicity, we seek to put our attention, money, and possessions to use in God's ways, showing what is really important to us. "For where your treasure is, there your heart will be also" (Matthew 6:21, Luke 12:34). Simplifying our lives helps us devote more time, talent, and treasure to what matters most in our lives—faith and relationship with God.

 Have you ever fasted? What do you think you might learn about yourself or God if you fasted for a period of time? How do your attention, money, and possessions show what is really important to you?

Simplicity and Asceticism

In the early church, the practice of *asceticism* attempted to strip off attachments to unspiritual things of this world. Many faithful Christians denied themselves to focus on more spiritual aspects. Some believers took this too far—denying themselves food or sleep for extended periods of time or hurting themselves (self-flagellation).

People in monastic orders often followed an ascetic life, so when monasticism grew in significance in the third century, asceticism grew also. Frequently monastics sought to separate from the rest of society as well, devoting themselves to prayer, fasting, and the study of scripture.

Simplicity and asceticism are related but different. Simplicity's purpose is similar to asceticism, but its philosophy and methods are different. Asceticism views everything outside the realms of church and faith as evil. For example, asceticism would ask you to rid yourself completely of knick-knacks, whereas simplicity would invite you to simplify your knick-knacks and make room for a spiritual reminder like a candle or a cross or a piece of religious art.

Did You Know?

• The Essenes were a second-century ascetic Jewish sect. They held possessions in common, wore white garments, and strictly observed the Sabbath. The Dead Sea scrolls were probably composed, copied, or collected by the Essenes.

 Why do you think asceticism moved away from public life into monasticism? Why can't we humans (in any age) seem to exercise moderation in our acquisition of goods?

Where Your Treasure Is...

Jennifer and David had been married for three years. Barely making ends meet, sometimes they had to decide which bills to pay. Between the cable bills, the cell phone bills, the credit card payments, the furniture bills, the restaurant tabs, and the expensive gym membership, there was never much left over.

Then Jennifer's workplace was downsized and she lost her job. She and David had to make some hard choices to cut back and simplify their expenses. They agreed to stop eating out. David gave up his iced espresso and Jennifer gave up her daily candy bar in the afternoon. Instead of going to the hair salon every week, Jennifer asked her friend Sue to do her hair once a month. Although they really liked movies, they cancelled the premium movie cable channels and spent more time watching library videos and DVDs.

Because they didn't have the money for extraneous purchases, Jennifer could no longer spend time in "retail therapy." Instead, she decided to comb through their belongings and find things that could be donated to charity. David cancelled his gym membership and they rode their bikes around the lake three times a week instead.

Because they couldn't afford to eat at restaurants, they decided to enroll in a Bible study at church on Wednesday nights. They found they also had more energy to attend worship on Sunday mornings when they hadn't been out the night before at the movie theater.

Wrap-up

Simplicity scales back our excesses and worldly distractions and invites us to experience what it means to have "enough." A lifestyle of simplicity is very compatible with the next practice, care of the earth.

 Think critically about how you spend your money, time, and energy. If you had to downsize your life and financial commitments, where would you begin? Why haven't you done that yet?

In My Life

- Serve a simple, no-fuss meal to family or friends. Focus on the people and enjoy the conversation.
- Look at your daily planner or calendar. What do your scheduling choices say about you?
- Think about your daily routine. Are prayer and scripture reading important to you? Is there something you could cut back to give you time to pursue prayer and scripture reading more intentionally?
- Give your time instead of purchasing a birthday or Christmas gift. "Coupons" for computer lessons, a movie marathon at home, babysitting, and so on can be priceless gifts.
- Look at your home and belongings. Do you have too much of any one thing? Is there someone else who could use this item? Is there anything that isn't important to you, but takes up a lot of space? If so, consider donating it or giving it to a friend.
- Ask yourself, "Do I really need this?" the next time something in your home breaks down and can't be repaired. If you can do without it, get rid of it rather than replacing it.
- Sort through your clothing to see if you can donate any items to charity.
- Go without a daily food or drink treat in order to sponsor a missionary.
- Give up an extraneous meeting or obligation to open up more time for faith practices.
- Talk with your family and friends about the ways you celebrate birthdays, Easter, Thanksgiving, Christmas, and other special occasions. Are any practices distracting you from the meaning of the celebration? How could simplifying enhance your celebration?

WORLD 1

World 2

How do we embrace the world?

Care of the Earth

Key Text: Psalm 24:1-2
Key Idea: Practicing care of the earth means treating the world as a gift from God.

Step-by-step: Care of the Earth

Preparation: none
Materials needed: none
Time: often just a few minutes

1 Pray for God's guidance in your care of the earth.

2 Consider what you can continue, change, or do differently to show care of the earth.

3 Carry out these ways of caring for the earth.

 Don't try to make too many earth-friendly life changes at once. Make changes gradually, building on your successes as you grow.

 How are you already practicing daily or weekly care of the earth? What prevents you from adopting additional earth-friendly practices?

Let's Start at the Very Beginning

The call for care of creation begins in the book of beginnings, Genesis. In Genesis 1:26 God states, "Let us make human-kind [the Hebrew word *adam*] in our image, according to our likeness; and let them have dominion over the fish of the sea, and over the birds of the air, and over the cattle, and over all the wild animals of the earth, and over every creeping thing that creeps upon the earth." The word "dominion" here isn't associated with "dominating." Instead the implication is that of "rule," treating all of creation as just and loving rulers would treat their subjects. When God gave dominion over creation to humans, God was saying, "I created something special, and I want you to care for it as I would care for you."

The importance of creation to the Creator is lifted up repeatedly in the Psalms. Psalm 24:1 reminds us that "The earth is the Lord's and all that is in it, the world, and those who live in it." Psalm 19:1 lets us know that the earth isn't just something fun to look at: "The heavens are telling the glory of God; and the firmament proclaims his handiwork."

The Bible also emphasizes the connection humans have with all creatures. In Genesis 2 we are told "the Lord God formed man from the dust of the ground" (verse 7). Then "out of the ground the Lord God made to grow every tree that is pleasant to the sight and good for food" (verse 9). Finally, "out of the ground the Lord God formed every ani-mal of the field and every bird of the air" (verse 19). All living things are connected, since we all come from the ground. That's why the writer of Ecclesiastes is able to proclaim, "For the fate of humans and the fate of animals is the same; as one dies, so dies the other. They all have the same breath, and humans have no advantage over the animals; for all is vanity. All go to one place; all are from the dust, and all turn to dust again" (3:19-20).

Why do you think God gave the earth over to our care? How do you feel about being connected to all of creation?

The Circle of Life

For most of history, humans have lived in harmony with creation. Everything needed for survival came from creation, so there was an understanding that the world must be treated with care and respect. There was also an understanding that humans and the earth are connected. Even our languages reflect that understanding. Genesis tells us that God created humans (*adam*) from the dust of the ground (*adamah*) (2:7). Even the English word *human* is "rooted" in the Latin word *humus* (topsoil)! For most of human history there was a strong people–ground connection.

At some point that connection weakened. Instead of living in harmony with nature, people began to focus on conquering nature. Instead of farming for the family, people farmed for money. Instead of using what was essential, we began to horde what we wanted.

St. Francis of Assisi, and others throughout the years, attempted to re-establish our connection with creation. St. Francis shared with all who would listen the importance creation has for us and for God. His love of creation was so strong that he even preached to the animals. Martin Luther emphasized the *adam-adamah* connection, reminding people that we are of humble origins. We, like all of creation, are of the earth. To think of ourselves as separate from creation, or better than creation, is a sin of pride.

In recent times many individuals, congregations, denominations, and ecumenical organizations have joined the chorus. For example, the Evangelical Lutheran Church in America (ELCA) adopted a social statement in 1993 stating, "Christian concern for the environment is shaped by the Word of God spoken in creation, the Love of God hanging on a cross, the Breath of God daily renewing the face of the earth." With so much happening to the earth in such a short time, the statement

Did You Know?

• It's estimated that 82 species become extinct *every day!* That's over 30,000 varieties of life lost every year. Before this modern extinction phase, one species became extinct every four years.

acknowledges that "the prospect of doing too little too late leads many people to despair. But as people of faith, captives of hope, and vehicles of God's promise, we face the crisis" (Department for Studies, Division for Church in Society, "Caring for Creation: Vision, Hope and Justice," 1993, Evangelical Lutheran Church in America).

 What do you think prompted the change from "care of creation" to "conquest of creation"? Do you believe Christians have done all that they can do for the care of the earth?

Happily Ever After

In 1987 the U.N. World Commission on Environment and Development encouraged the world to work toward sustainable development. Sustainable development means meeting the needs of the present without compromising the ability of future generations to meet their own needs.

St. Olaf College in Northfield, Minnesota, is striving for sustainability. In 2003 the school published "Sustaining St. Olaf," highlighting a commitment to economic and ecological sustainability. The report included an audit of current projects, guidelines for designing green buildings, and "Sustainability Principles" for the future.

St. Olaf's operations are actively moving toward sustainability. These are some of the steps that have been taken:

- Reducing the amount of energy used on campus.
- Producing clean energy with a wind turbine that generates one-third of the school's electricity.
- Installing a composter that converts all food waste into food for the school's gardens and agricultural lands.

Wrap-up

We are connected to the earth and all of its creatures. When we practice care of the earth, we do as God commanded. God also calls us to the next faith practice, justice.

 There are many small things you can do to make a difference in the care of the earth. Little things done by thousands—or even millions—of people will make a big difference.

In My Life

- Take the stairs instead of the elevator.
- Save paper that has been printed on only one side for scrap or note paper, or print items for your personal use on the other side of the paper. Save ink by setting the default print quality on printers to draft or economy mode and the default color to black. Recycle ink cartridges too.
- Turn off lights when you leave a room.
- Turn off computer monitors and put computers in "hibernate" mode when not in use.
- Read more about St. Olaf College's ongoing journey at www.stolaf.edu/green.
- Consider ways to reduce your use of fuel. Walk, ride a bike, or take public transportation whenever you can.
- Learn about your community's recycling programs and take advantage of these opportunities.
- Encourage your friends, family members, and neighbors to practice care of the earth.

World 3

How do we embrace the world?

Justice

Key Text: Isaiah 56:1-2
Key Idea: Biblical justice involves practical actions to watch over the weak, provide for the poor, welcome the stranger, and uplift the underprivileged.

Step-by-step: Justice

In the Bible, justice is active and involves taking care of the needs of people who are weak, poor, and underprivileged.
Preparation: none
Materials needed: none
Time: 5-50 minutes

1 Begin each day with a prayer asking for God's guidance in doing justice.

2 Actively look for instances where biblical justice is missing or not apparent as you go through your day. This may include homelessness, poverty, racism, sexism, ageism, prejudice, and stereotyping.

3 Find ways to respond on your own and support organizations working to alleviate these issues.

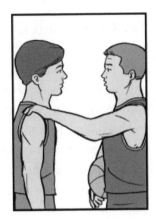

4 Pray for each situation you noted during the day.

 You might see many areas where biblical justice is needed, but start small. Focus on one or two justice issues and give your all to them.

 Is it easy to spot areas lacking biblical justice? How do you usually respond to justice issues?

Let Justice Roll Down!

Biblical justice is very different from what most people consider justice today. Biblical justice isn't about guilty people getting what they deserve. It's about making sure that those who are disadvantaged are taken care of. It's not about what has been done to you; it's about what you do for others. God established a way of living for God's chosen people after they left Egypt, instructing, "You shall not wrong or oppress a resident alien, for you were aliens in the land of Egypt. You shall not abuse any widow or orphan. . . . If you lend money to my people, to the poor among you, you shall not deal with them as a creditor; you shall not exact interest from them" (Exodus 22:21-22, 25). Justice isn't biblical justice unless it watches over the weak, provides for the poor, is sympathetic to the stranger, and uplifts the underprivileged.

Biblical justice isn't passive or neutral. Amos makes this clear when he says, "Let justice roll down like waters, and righteousness like an ever-flowing stream" (Amos 5:24). Micah reminds us that for God, the emphasis isn't on rituals or material items. God isn't focused on burnt offerings, thousands of rams, or rivers of oil. God isn't even concerned about you giving your firstborn over to the Lord (Micah 6:6-7). But God does require us to *do* justice, *love* kindness, and *walk* humbly with God (Micah 6:8, emphasis added).

The book of James echoes the emphasis on justice being active: "What good is it, my brothers and sisters, if you say

you have faith but do not have works?
Can faith save you? If a brother or sister
is naked and lacks daily food, and one
of you says to them, 'Go in peace; keep
warm and eat your fill,' and yet you do
not supply their bodily needs, what is
the good of that? So faith by itself, if it
has no works, is dead" (2:14-17). This is
not works righteousness; we are saved
by grace through faith. But that faith should bear fruit.

Biblical justice is about having a right relationship with
God, other humans, and the earth. Isaiah put it this way,
"Thus says the LORD: Maintain justice, and do what is right,
for soon my salvation will come, and my deliverance be
revealed" (56:1). As Christians we are called to maintain justice and do what is right. Not what is right (just) for us, but
what is right (just) for those around us.

*How would you determine what is right (just) for oth-
ers? How can you respond to justice issues? How can
your congregation respond?*

...And Justice for All

We're all familiar with contemporary justice. We hear it in sound bites on the evening news after the verdict has been read in a criminal trial. The prosecution or the victim is eager to tell the world that "justice has been served." Although we might refer to this as contemporary justice, this understanding of justice dates back to Hammurabi, the Babylonian king. Hammurabi laid out a precise code (law) that regulated how a society should be organized.

Although this is not the oldest code set forth, it is the one that has had the most impact on ancient and modern societies. Every negative action (e.g., robbery, bearing false witness, accidental death) warranted a grim retaliatory punishment.

Biblical justice appears in the Pentateuch (the first five books of the Bible), but it doesn't get a real workout until much later. Many of the prophets bring up the issue of justice before and during the Jewish exile. The people are reminded that as an oppressed people, there will come a time when they will be lifted up out of the social-political pit they are in. But they are also reminded that just because they have it bad doesn't mean they should treat others poorly. God calls the people to "Maintain justice, and do what is right" (Isaiah 56:1).

Jesus placed a strong emphasis on biblical justice (Matthew 23:23). Yet somewhere along the way justice for Christians turned into "just us." Many people believe that if those who are poor, weak, or disenfranchised don't have all that they need, it's because they haven't done what is needed to deserve it. The biblical concept of justice, however, calls us to give people what they need even when this means giving them what they don't "deserve."

How have you defined justice in the past? Has your view changed over the years? Who is in need of biblical justice in your community and in the world?

Connecting Church and Community

Many people believe that the church should not get involved with political issues. As far as the Bible is concerned, however, there is not a separation between church and community. If there were, Moses would not have advocated for God's people and led them out of Egypt.

The ONE campaign seeks to decrease global poverty 50% by 2015 and advocates against HIV/AIDS, hunger, and homelessness. More than 2 million Americans had signed the ONE declaration as of April 2007. Partners in this campaign include several religious groups and denominations.

Student-led advocacy teams at some ELCA campus ministries, universities, and seminaries have participated in the ONE campaign. Members of these advocacy teams have found the work is not always easy but is rewarding. Some teams have encountered strong resistance, while others have received support and encouragement.

Wrap-up

When we strive to have a right (just) relationship with God, other people, and the world, the practice of justice comes naturally. Doing justice often calls for service to the larger community and world, our next faith practice.

The practice of justice is often more rewarding when you carry it out with other people.

In My Life

- Think about your attitudes and actions toward people of different ages, abilities, social positions, economic levels, ethnic backgrounds, and so on.
- Write a letter to the editor of your local paper about a justice issue that's been overlooked in your community.
- Look for groups and organizations advocating for justice in your neighborhood, congregation, community, and in the world. Join one that fits your interests and passions—or start your own group.
- Write to your elected representatives regarding a justice issue you feel strongly about.
- Pray for people who are poor, hungry, abused, or disadvantaged in other ways.
- Consider what you will say or do the next time you hear a comment that stereotypes you or someone else.
- Welcome someone who is new to your neighborhood, congregation, school, or workplace.

World 4

How do we embrace the world?

Service to the Larger Community and World

Key Text: John 13:34-35
Key Idea: When we serve the larger community and world, we live out Jesus' command to love one another.

Step-by-step: Service to the Larger Community and World

Preparation: none
Materials needed: none
Time: a few minutes or longer

1 Consider places where you might have a service opportunity in the community or world.

Identify one act of service to do. Continue to look for opportunities to serve in your community or world.

 Don't overlook things you already do but might not think of as acts of service, like shoveling an elderly neighbor's sidewalk or donating to a hunger relief organization.

How can you maintain the dignity of the people you serve while meeting a need they have? Who are some people who serve you on a regular basis? Have you expressed your gratitude to them recently?

Selfless Service in the Gospels

In the New Testament, Jesus speaks about serving in such a way that our deeds are not seen by others (Matthew 6:1). Every charitable act doesn't need to be anonymous, but we must not do charitable acts in order to be honored by others. Jesus also taught that servanthood is what matters in the end. In Matthew 20:25-28, Luke 22:26-27, and Mark 10:42-45, he indicates that the Son of Man came to serve and whoever wishes to be first must be slave of all. These are hard words to our modern ears, but they invite us to change our attitude toward service.

In Matthew 25:31-46, Jesus tells a story of two different groups of people and what will happen when the Son of Man comes in his glory. One group fed the hungry, gave drink to the thirsty, welcomed the stranger, clothed the naked, cared for the sick, and visited the prisoner. The other group did not. When confronted by the Son of Man, both groups are surprised to learn that whenever they served others, they were serving Jesus.

The story of the good Samaritan in Luke 10:25-37 gives another example of selfless service. The Samaritan man who found the robbery victim committed to helping in any way possible. Jesus uses this example to show that seeking

Did You Know?

• When we serve others, we may expect overt expressions of gratitude from the ones we serve, but Christians serve because of love, not in order to get recognition.

opportunities to serve and to minister to those around us is part and parcel of discipleship.

One of Jesus' final acts before his crucifixion was washing his disciples' feet (John 13). Washing feet would have been a menial task, better left to someone with less dignity and social standing. But Jesus wanted to show his disciples that the posture of a Christian is the posture of a servant. Jesus hoped that they would learn from his example, inviting them to wash one another's feet (John 13:14).

 Why should we serve others? Can you stoop to serve without being downtrodden?

Charity and Servanthood

Christian servanthood grows from a desire to imitate our Lord Jesus Christ, who came not to be served, but to serve. Biblical service means willingly giving of one's self on behalf of another person. We choose to give of our time or money to another person in need or an organization that serves those in need.

Christian service in the world can take many forms. The most prevalent and obvious is charity or almsgiving, the giving of money or food to a person in need (or an organization that benefits those in need). Most forms of charity are concerned with providing food, water, clothing, and shelter, and caring for those who are sick.

Many Christians throughout history have shown what it means to do good deeds of kindness, sacrificing personal time and resources for others without ever expecting to be repaid. In the 1600s, Vincent de Paul, a Catholic priest, generously devoted his life to helping people who were poor. In many cities today, you can find a St. Vincent de Paul Society still helping those who are poor.

In your own community, many Christians have provided charity or founded charitable organizations. If you investigate, you may find that hospitals, food pantries, counseling centers, orphanages, schools, nursing homes, and so on were started by Christians who sought to provide service to the world through the ministry of a non-profit organization.

By serving others, we honor them as valued children of God. It's easy to view others as needy or ungrateful when we offer an act of service, but true Christian service grows out of a commitment to love others and show love through our actions. Our acts of service in the world acknowledge that we have been commanded to serve one another and are therefore responsible to care for one another.

Did You Know?

• Your community or denomination has service organizations that are seeking volunteers or donations. Lutheran World Relief, for example, works with partners in 35 countries to help people grow food, improve health, strengthen communities, end conflict, build livelihoods, and recover from disasters.

Can you name some famous Christians who lived out servanthood and charity? Tell about someone you know who lives out servanthood and charity.

WWYD: What Would You Do?

As we reflect on service, it's important to acknowledge that there are many ways of serving others. Consider for a moment the story of Joe, an unemployed veteran who stands outside the grocery store asking for help.

- One person may respond to Joe by pulling out a couple bucks and hurriedly stuffing it in his hand.
- Someone might nod hello to Joe, saying that they can't help at this time, but go home and write a check to the local social service agency that works with veterans.
- Another might stop and talk to Joe, offering to pray for him by name at church and expressing gratitude for his years of service.
- Yet another may walk right past Joe, but use the encounter as a reminder to purchase non-perishables for the church food pantry.
- Perhaps one person would offer to purchase Joe food from the store, perhaps letting him pick out some items in order to let him decide what he really needs.

- Another person could go home and look up information about how to advocate against hunger and fight for those who are hungry throughout the world.
- Somebody else might use their encounter with Joe as a reminder to go to a neighbor's home the next day and offer to cut the lawn while a family member is serving in the military overseas.

Wrap-up

Service to the larger community and world can be provided through an individual (helping a neighbor) or an organization (volunteering at a food pantry). Christian service invites us into relationship with others by meeting a need. The next faith practice, sharing the story, also invites us into relationship with others.

 **PS** Christian service means using your gifts to serve your neighbor. Service is a way of giving of yourself, not to be rewarded but to honor what you have already been given.

In My Life

- Look for simple, small ways to serve others in your community, such as free babysitting for a neighbor with kids, baking cookies for the fire station, or buying a meal for a homeless person.
- Serve with family members or friends at food pantries, homeless shelters, soup kitchens, nursing homes, hospitals, and social service organizations. (Many of these organizations welcome volunteers of all ages, so take the opportunity to encourage a young person to serve.)
- Make service something that you live rather than a special event in your life. Strive to give of yourself to others as a way to honor the gifts that God has given you. When someone asks for your assistance, ask yourself "Why shouldn't I?" instead of "Why should I?"
- Consider ways that you can use your gifts to serve others. Find something that you are good at, and then reflect on how that could help another person or organization. Go beyond the obvious. Almost any skill can be utilized to serve some group of people in need.

World 5

How do we embrace the world?

Sharing the Story

Key Text: Romans 10:14-17
Key Idea: Sharing the story means sharing where our story intersects Jesus' story.

Step-by-step: Sharing the Story

Preparation: minimal
Materials needed: none
Time: 5 minutes

1
Look for someone to talk to and an opportunity to share.

2
Share your faith story—the story of what God has done and is doing in your life.

3 Continuously look for opportunities to share your story.

DIY Remember that you are not trying to convert your hearers. Sharing the story is like planting a seed, but God gives the growth.

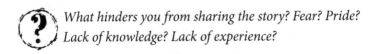

What hinders you from sharing the story? Fear? Pride? Lack of knowledge? Lack of experience?

I Love to Tell the Story

Sharing the story may feel scary at first. However, Jesus said that we should not worry about what we are going to say, "for it is not you who speak, but the Spirit of your Father speaking through you" (Matthew 10:20). God will help us know what to say at the right time. The disciples were afraid after the crucifixion and hid out of fear (John 20:19). Even after they saw the resurrected Lord ascend into heaven, they kept to themselves (Acts 1). But on the day of Pentecost, after the Holy Spirit had come upon the believers, they went out among the people, and Peter proclaimed the story with boldness (Acts 2).

Sharing the story has never been easy. The early Christians faced hardships and persecution for sharing the story. Stephen was compelled to tell the story, even though it cost him his life (Acts 7). Paul was scorned and imprisoned but shared the story with all who would hear.

Although we don't face the same persecution, we seem even more hesitant than the early Christians when it comes to sharing the story. But sharing the story isn't about converting people to Christianity or getting them to join your church. It's about planting the seed and allowing God to produce the harvest.

Did You Know?

• You can share the story in ordinary times and places—over dinner; instead of watching TV in the evening; while you watch kids play at a playground, wait for an appointment, or walk the dog.

Who first shared the story with you? How did they do this? Who watered the seeds and helped them grow?

On a Mission from God

Early on, sharing the story was a way of maintaining the faith in an oral culture. With no easy access to books, it was important for each individual to pass along the story to the next generation. In the Old Testament, God instructed the people to share the faith with those who followed (Deuteronomy 6:1-9). Sharing the story in that culture was inwardly focused, strengthening the faithful and deepening the faith of those who already believed.

Jesus called his followers to be witnesses, sharing the gospel story with all people on earth. He commanded, "Go therefore and make disciples of all nations" (Matthew 28:19) and "you will be my witnesses in Jerusalem, in all Judea and Samaria, and to the ends of the earth" (Acts 1:8).

For much of Christian history, the church used these passages as justification for spreading God's mission through coercion (either subtly, as in the early missionaries during the colonial period, or violently, as in the Inquisition). As recently as the late twentieth century, sharing the story was seen as converting nonbelievers from their "pagan" ways.

Today, under an accompaniment model for mission, missionaries build and strengthen indigenous churches, rather

WORLD 5

than founding new ministries. They share the story in many locations—in schools, hospitals, farms, marketplaces, and through local community development.

We are all called to the mission of the church. That doesn't mean we all must travel to foreign lands and meet exotic people. We can be missionaries in our own schools, workplaces, and neighborhoods. We do this by sharing the story—our story—just as the early church shared its story.

How could you share the story in your daily life? How do you develop a level of trust with people so that they will listen to you when you share the story?

Just a Little Faith

As Evan heard his pastor's sermon on sharing the story, he silently rolled his eyes. "Of course you would say that," he thought. "You're the pastor. It doesn't work like that in my life." As he left, he shook the pastor's hand and said "Good sermon," though he couldn't remember much of it.

On Monday, Michael, a coworker, confided in Evan that he was diagnosed with prostate cancer. "Wow," Evan exclaimed, "that's tough news."

"Yeah," Michael replied, "and the doctor recommends surgery. You had heart surgery last year, how did you make it through?"

"I prayed a lot," Evan answered. "And I don't know what I would have done without my church. I'll keep you in my prayers. Can I also put you on our church's prayer list?"

During lunch Evan went to the bank. The person in front of him was yelling at the teller, saying how incompetent she was. When the customer left and Evan approached the window, it was obvious that she was hurt. "You know," Evan started, "I'm always thankful for how professional and courteous you are. I hope your day gets better." "Thanks," she responded. As Evan walked away, he turned around and said to her, "Have a blessed day," noticing a smile on her face.

Later as he and his wife talked, Evan shared both of these stories with her. "Isn't that what Pastor Sarah was preaching? Sharing your story?" she asked. "I guess it is," Evan said, "but I thought it would be harder than that."

Wrap-up

We share the story by using our own experiences and describing where our story and Jesus' story intersect. We plant the seeds, and God produces the harvest.

PS Don't sit around planning or rehearsing the best way to share the story or it will come out sounding like a canned speech. The best thing is to share from your heart.

Our faith invites us to engage with everything around us. God's call doesn't remove us from the world. It draws us into relationship with those around us. Being committed to God's mission, we embrace the world.

By embracing the world, we celebrate the church. We become a disciple by experiencing God working actively in our lives. And we cannot do any of these things without discovering the Bible and what it means for our lives.

In My Life

- Take time every day to notice all the blessings that God has poured out on you. It's easier to share your story when you notice all that God has done for you.
- Pray before meals when gathering with family and friends plus when you eat in a restaurant.
- Look for opportunities in the workplace or school to speak about the way God works in your life. Explain your decisions as they relate to your faith values.
- Keep your Faith Practices cards handy to encourage you as you go through the week.
- Listen and offer to pray for a friend who is experiencing a difficult time. If your faith has sustained you in times of distress, share your story as a way of encouraging this person.
- Invite someone to attend worship with you.
- Tell someone how this Faith Practices course has encouraged your faith to grow.